Overcoming Emotional Abuse

Susan Elliot-Wright is a freelance writer. She trained as a magazine journalist, writing hundreds of articles for newspapers and magazines, as well as four health information books for teenagers and the following books for Sheldon Press: *Coping with Type 2 Diabetes* (2006), *Living with Heart Failure* (2006), *Overcoming Insomnia* (2008), *Coping with Epilepsy in Children and Young People* (2009) and *Overcoming Emotional Abuse* (second edn, 2016). She now focuses mainly on fiction. Her first novel, *The Things We Never Said*, was published in 2013, and her second, *The Secrets We Left Behind*, in 2014, both by Simon & Schuster. Her third novel, as yet untitled, will be published in early 2017, and she is currently working on her fourth. She lives in Sheffield with her husband.

Overcoming Common Problems Series

Selected titles

A full list of titles is available from Sheldon Press,
36 Causton Street, London SW1P 4ST and on our website at
www.sheldonpress.co.uk

Overcoming Common Problems Series

Overcoming Common Problems Series

Overcoming Common Problems

Overcoming Emotional Abuse
Survive and heal

Second edition

SUSAN ELLIOT-WRIGHT

First published in Great Britain in 2007

Sheldon Press
36 Causton Street
London SW1P 4ST
www.sheldonpress.co.uk

Second edition published 2016

British Library Cataloguing-in-Publication Data
A catalogue record for this book is available from the British Library

ISBN 978-1-84709-405-6
eBook ISBN 978-1-84709-406-3

Typeset by Fakenham Prepress Solutions, Fakenham, Norfolk NR21 8NN
First printed in Great Britain by Ashford Colour Press
Subsequently digitally reprinted in Great Britain

eBook by Fakenham Prepress Solutions, Fakenham, Norfolk NR21 8NN

Produced on paper from sustainable forests

Contents

Acknowledgements

The women I interviewed while writing this book told of misery and sadness, of fear and hopelessness, and of severe mental and physical pain; some of their stories kept me awake at night. I have not included all of these accounts, but most that do appear are typical. I hope the courage and determination shown by these women in moving on and making new lives for themselves and their children will be a source of inspiration to others. I would like to thank them for sharing their stories with me, and to wish them the future happiness they deserve. I would also like to thank my own family for their love and support, my children for helping me through the worst, and my husband for showing me what it's supposed to be like.

Introduction

When we hear about abusive relationships, we tend to think of physical violence – 'the battered wife'; less well known, but at least as common, is psychological, verbal and emotional abuse. Specific definitions of this type of abuse and how to recognize it will be discussed in detail in Chapter 1, but generally the term applies where one person persistently causes severe mental pain to another by the use of fear, intimidation, humiliation and manipulation. Physical abuse may follow on from this, or it may not come at all, but even without broken bones, split lips, black eyes and pulled-out hair, the abused woman will be deeply scarred by her experience and may take years to recover.

This type of abuse can occur between parents and children, between siblings or even at work, but this book will concentrate on psychological, verbal and emotional abuse within marriage and similar relationships. In the majority of abusive partner relationships, it is the woman who is being abused and references in this book to the abuser as 'he' and the abused as 'she' reflect this. However, if you're a man who is being abused by a male or female partner, the information and advice here should be useful for you, too.

Non-physical abuse is insidious; it wears down the victim over time so that, eventually, not only has she lost her confidence and self-esteem to such an extent that she may feel she deserves the treatment she's receiving, but she may no longer trust her own judgement enough to realize what is happening to her. Many women in emotionally abusive relationships, just like those suffering from physical abuse, start to blame themselves. This is how the abuser works: if he can make you doubt your own perceptions, you will be easier to control and less likely to challenge him. If you don't challenge him, the abuse increases, making you even more vulnerable and so on – it's a vicious circle. Chapter 2 will look in more detail at the effects of non-physical abuse and how it can damage your health and other relationships.

The key to dealing with and surviving emotional abuse is recognizing, understanding and accepting that what is happening *is* abuse and that it's not your fault. Once you accept this, you are in a stronger position to make the decision whether to challenge the abuse and attempt to repair the relationship or whether you need to end it and begin your recovery after it is over. Leaving a long-term relationship is an incredibly difficult decision to make, especially when you are no longer sure of your own judgement, but for some women, myself included, it really is the only way to escape the abuse and begin rebuilding your life. My own story is still painful to relive, even 16 years on, but like most of the other true stories you will read in this book, it has a happy ending.

I finally left my marriage after 12 years. If I am honest, the signs were there even before we were married. He was jealous, possessive, moody, critical and short-tempered. I was initially flattered by his jealousy – I thought he must really, really love me. But he seemed to be always angry, and when I asked what was wrong, he'd snap, 'Nothing.' I cried a lot, but thought if I could just do things properly and love him enough, it would be all right. It wasn't. I tried to make it work, but it seemed I couldn't do anything right.

The first time I seriously thought of leaving was five years after we married, when I was expecting our second child. I didn't drive in those days and so, unwilling to visit my family with me, my husband had dropped me and our 13-month-old daughter at my mum's while he went for 'a quick pint'. He promised to be back by 8 p.m. so I could get the baby to bed and have an early night myself, as I was in the last stages of pregnancy. I didn't expect him to be on time – he never was – but 9 p.m. came and went, and so did 10 p.m. I was desperate to get home; I was tired, the baby was crying and my parents had gone to bed after I'd assured them he'd be back at any minute. When he arrived at 10.45, I was waiting with my coat on by the front door, the baby in my arms and the folded buggy next to me. I complained, reminding him that he'd said 8 p.m. He went into one of his familiar rages, silent but terrifying. He hurled the buggy down the concrete steps into the street, threw the changing bag into the car so violently that most of the contents spilled out, then he got in and sat revving the engine while I struggled to strap my crying daughter into her baby seat. I got in, and while I was trying to fasten the seatbelt over my eight-and-a-half-month bump, he accelerated away with a screech of tyres. The 15-minute drive home was a nightmare. He drove recklessly, way above the speed limit and barely slowing to take corners. His jaw was rigid, his face dark with fury. I was too afraid to move or speak and I sat petrified, tears streaming down my face, wondering if we'd get home alive.

When we arrived home, he got out, slammed the car door and went into the house, leaving me to gather myself, the baby and the scattered contents of the changing bag. He didn't speak to me at all that night, nor indeed for the next few days. The whole episode was not unusual.

What was the matter with me, you ask. Why didn't I get a cab instead of putting myself, my daughter and my unborn child at risk by getting into the car with a man who'd been drinking and who I knew would probably use his driving to display his anger and to frighten me further into submission? Many other abused women will know why: I was absolutely cowed by this man. I was unable to challenge him, unable to stand up for myself and terrified of what would happen if I did. Things were getting worse and I was becoming increasingly miserable. Could I leave him? The thought flashed through my mind. But where would I go with two babies under two? And, anyway, maybe things would improve when the baby came. I just needed not to upset him, not to complain, then perhaps it would be all right.

I stuck it for another seven years, during which time he criticized and humiliated me in front of people, shouted at me or, worse, refused to speak for long periods (three weeks, once). He criticized my friends and family, only allowing me to see them for short periods; he ridiculed my opinions, told me what to wear, how to have my hair and when I could and couldn't leave the house. He was moody and aggressive, snapping at me when he spoke, ignoring me if *I* spoke. He wanted constant attention, once tearing up a book because I was reading instead of talking to him. He shouted, slammed doors and banged things around so much that to this day I remain unusually sensitive to noise. He also wanted me to show 'affection' – not easy while he was looking at me as though he loathed and detested me, speaking to me through gritted teeth and jabbing his finger in my face. And there was more; much, much more.

So what happened? Eventually, after several people commented on his behaviour (he got careless, forgetting to behave differently in company), I began to realize that this was way beyond the ups and downs of a normal relationship, and in fact that the love I had once felt had been completely eroded. One of the things that helped me to realize this was, ironically, relationship counselling. I'd suggested this as a last attempt to save our marriage 'for the sake of the children'. I now wish we'd got away sooner. We had several sessions of counselling, and after each one the abuse became worse, leaving me a sobbing, tear-sodden mess. One day, I went to see the counsellor on my own, to thank her for her help but also to tell her that it wasn't working. I'd got to the stage where I'd begun to fantasize about him leaving me, meeting someone else and asking for a divorce. When he stayed out until the early hours, as he often did, I no longer worried that something bad had happened to him; if I'm honest, I sometimes rather hoped it had. The counsellor put her hand on my arm. 'You have tried hard,' she said. 'But if you don't get out of that marriage, you are going to shrivel up and die.'

That was the first time I really believed it wasn't my fault.

I took the two children and two black bin bags, one full of clothes, one full of toys, and I left him, filing for divorce soon after. He contested the divorce (thus further maintaining his control) so we had to go to court. My barrister made much of the fact that, shortly before I left, my husband had put his hands around my throat and banged my head on the floor – I remember looking up at the dog, who sat trembling under the table while this was happening. But this incident, while painful and frightening, was nothing compared to the mental pain and misery he'd inflicted on me over the years. Physical abuse horrifies people so much more than non-physical abuse, and yet non-physical abuse can be just as damaging, and even life-threatening when women start to consider suicide as the only means of escape.

The first few years after I left my husband were tough; he stalked and harassed me on and off for three years – controlling people don't like to let you go. But away from him I grew stronger, regained my confidence and self-respect, made new friends and went back to college. After taking GCSEs, then A levels, I went on to gain a good honours degree in English and to train as a journalist. In the final year of my degree I met the man who is now my husband. I now know what a loving relationship is, how it should nurture and nourish both partners through love, friendship, mutual respect and mutual support.

In the following pages, you will find definitions of emotional and psychological abuse (Chapter 1), the damage it can cause (Chapter 2) and possible explanations as to why it might happen, together with examples of who is most likely to abuse or to be abused (Chapter 3). Obviously, the levels of abuse vary, as do the possible causes and backgrounds of those concerned. It may, in some cases, be possible to stop the abuse and repair the relationship, and Chapter 4 looks at this possibility. In many cases, though, the only solution is to end the relationship. Chapter 5 looks at how you might make this difficult and painful decision, as well as offering practical advice on how to go about it. Recovering from an abusive relationship can take many years, and may be hindered by continuing attempts by your ex to control you even once you've left him. Chapter 6 looks at this difficult period and how to cope with potential problems.

Throughout the book, as well as referring to my own experiences I have quoted a number of women who have suffered emotional, verbal, psychological and, in some cases, physical abuse at the hands of their partners. In Chapter 7, you will read more stories, in more detail (names and some identifying details have been changed). These accounts are sometimes difficult to read, but are frequently inspiring as we see how the women have courageously overcome the problems and difficulties they have experienced as a result of the abuse they have suffered.

I hope that this book, with the inclusion of my own experience and that of the women who generously agreed to talk to me about theirs, will be of some help in raising awareness of this widespread but little-talked-about problem.

I wish all those reading this book the very best of luck, strength and courage in dealing with and recovering from the trauma caused to them and their children by the abusive relationship in their lives. I hope that you will find true happiness and fulfilment in the future, as many of us have.

Note: Some agencies regard the term 'victim' as unhelpful in describing someone who has experienced abuse, preferring 'survivor'. After some deliberation, I have decided to stick with 'victim' because I do not feel that it implies passivity and helplessness in the woman, but rather that it emphasizes her complete lack of blame and responsibility for what is happening to her. I also feel it is more appropriate for women who are still in abusive relationships and who may not necessarily recognize their partner's behaviour as abuse.

1

What is emotional abuse?

Abuse that is non-physical – i.e. emotional, psychological and verbal – is very difficult to recognize. There are no black eyes, no cut and swollen lips, no mysteriously broken bones; but the damage can be as great and the scarring as deep as that resulting from a physically abusive relationship. In fact, Women's Aid, the charity set up in 1974 to offer support and protection to women fleeing abusive relationships, lists many of the types of behaviours discussed in this book as forms of domestic violence, even where there is no actual physical abuse.

Women's Aid defines domestic violence as:

- destructive criticism and verbal abuse: shouting; mocking; accusing; name-calling; verbally threatening;
- pressure tactics: sulking; threatening to withhold money, disconnect the telephone, take the car away, commit suicide, take the children away, report you to welfare agencies unless you comply with his demands regarding bringing up the children; lying to your friends and family about you; telling you that you have no choice in any decisions;
- disrespect: persistently putting you down in front of other people; not listening or responding when you talk; interrupting your telephone calls; taking money from your purse without asking; refusing to help with childcare or housework;
- breaking trust: lying to you; withholding information from you; being jealous; having other relationships; breaking promises and shared agreements;
- isolation: monitoring or blocking your telephone calls; telling

you where you can and cannot go; preventing you from
seeing friends and relatives;
- harassment: following you; checking up on you; opening your
  mail; repeatedly checking to see who has telephoned you;
  embarrassing you in public;
- threats: making angry gestures; using physical size to intimidate; shouting you down; destroying your possessions;
  breaking things; punching walls; wielding a knife or a gun;
  threatening to kill or harm you and the children;
- sexual violence: using force, threats or intimidation to make
  you perform sexual acts; having sex with you when you don't
  want to have sex; any degrading treatment based on your
  sexual orientation;
- physical violence: punching; slapping; hitting; biting; pinch-
  ing; kicking; pulling hair out; pushing; shoving; burning;
  strangling;
- denial: saying the abuse doesn't happen; saying you caused
  the abusive behaviour; being publicly gentle and patient; crying and begging for forgiveness; saying it will never happen
  again.

(This list is provided with the kind permission of the Women's
Aid Federation of England <www.womensaid.org.uk>.)

Basically, then, non-physical abuse is when one person persistently causes another to experience severe mental anguish, fear
and distress. The ways in which the abuser achieves this are
looked at in more detail later, but his aim, either consciously or
unconsciously, is always the same: to dominate and control his
victim.

Emotionally and psychologically abusive men, like those
who are physically violent, may be careful to cover their tracks.
They are often charming in public and express absolute disgust
and outrage when they hear about men who hurt their wives
physically. The abuse can seem subtle, especially if you take

each incident separately – nobody would say that everyone who occasionally shouts at or criticizes their partner is an abuser: we all snap at each other now and then, or criticize something the other has done or said. But if someone does this *persistently*, particularly if it seems to be a one-way thing – he shouts at or criticizes her, but she never shouts at or criticizes him – it could well be an indication of an abusive relationship.

The fact that it is so hard to spot – even when you're the one being abused – is one of the reasons it's difficult to do anything about. First, the notion that you can be abused without knowing it sounds absurd: if you don't recognize it, surely it can't be abuse? It can. The problem is that women who are suffering this type of abuse often convince themselves that the way their partner treats them is normal. This may be due to a reluctance to admit that something is badly wrong with the relation- ship – it is difficult to accept this, especially when they still love the person who is causing them such pain. Or it may be that their partner has managed to make them think his behaviour is normal: 'Any man would complain if...' or 'It's not just me – ask anyone.' He knows, of course, that she won't.

Second, even if they accept that the way their partner treats them is not normal, they may convince themselves that they deserve this treatment, and so they blame themselves for mak- ing their partner angry. Chapter 3 looks at possible reasons for this, but suffice to say that when a woman is being constantly told that she is stupid, neurotic, oversensitive, paranoid and so on, it is very difficult for her to then challenge the person criticizing her. As a result, she simply tries to do and be what he wants in order to minimize his aggression. This will not work, of course, because there was nothing wrong with her behaviour in the first place – she cannot win.

So what specific types of behaviour constitute non-physical abuse? As stated in the Introduction, this book focuses on abuse within marriage and similar relationships. However, many of these behaviours are typical of all abusers, simply taking a slightly different form depending on the nature of the relationship – whether it's parent–child, sibling–sibling, employer–employee and so on. It is difficult to categorize these behaviours precisely because, given that all are controlling and abusive and all are damaging to the victim's self-esteem, there is inevitably some crossover. Broadly speaking, however, emotionally and psychologically abusive behaviour falls into three main categories:

- controlling behaviour;
- wearing away of confidence and self-esteem;
- verbal abuse.

Controlling behaviour

In a sense, all abuse is controlling, but there are some specific behaviours that demonstrate this more than others. A man who exhibits controlling behaviour is often jealous and possessive. Jealousy itself may not appear to be a problem in the early stages of a relationship; it may even seem quite flattering when he says he feels jealous if you talk to someone else. But whereas a little sexual jealousy may be normal in a new relationship, unfounded jealousy and suspicion that continues and causes arguments or causes you to change your behaviour is not normal.

He may not 'allow' you to talk to other men, or to attend any social function without him, saying either that he doesn't trust you or that he doesn't trust other men. He may control what you wear, forbidding you to wear anything he considers revealing or provocative. If you challenge him, he'll say he's simply trying to protect you, or that he's 'naturally' worried because he loves you so much. He is quite likely to blame you for his behaviour, saying he wouldn't feel jealous if only you didn't give him cause. So you try to make things better by not giving him cause – not going out, not talking to other men and so on. But this will not make any difference because the jealousy is unreasonable and is masking the real reason for his behaviour – the need to dominate, to be in control and to have power over you.

Rather than forbidding you to wear revealing clothes, he may insist you dress in an overtly sexy way even if you're not comfortable with this. Charlotte's husband berated her for wearing jeans and told her that if she really loved him, she'd dress to please him, the way she had when they'd started going out together.

Charlotte

He used to constantly hark back to when we were first together, saying that I always used to wear sexy clothes but now I just dressed in any old rags because I didn't care about him any more. I tried to explain that it was different before we were married. We'd go out to clubs and bars and stuff, and yes, I did dress up for him. But that was when I was 25, out for a good time and trying to attract a mate. After we got married, I gave up work to have children and, to be honest, when you're spending the day caring for two kids under five the most convenient thing to wear is jeans. But he seemed to expect me to wear a short skirt and stiletto heels to do the housework.

He started to bring home all this stuff for me to wear – tight, tarty-looking dresses, stockings and suspenders, basques, even rubber stuff. It's not that I'm against sexy clothing – I love sexy underwear – but this stuff seemed a bit pervy. The thing is, I did actually wear it. I was so desperate to please him, I did what he asked. I'd get up in the morning, see to the kids and then put on full make-up, a skirt or dress and high heels. After he'd gone to work, I'd change into jeans and then put it all back on before he came home. It seems crazy, I know, but I kept thinking that if I could just get it right, he'd stop being angry with me and everything would be fine. But even when I wore the clothes he wanted me to wear, he'd get annoyed because I didn't look happy enough wearing them. I couldn't win.

Charlotte's experience is typical. She couldn't please her husband because his desire to control her was so great that when he succeeded in dictating what she wore, he then moved on to wanting to control her facial expression. If she'd managed to look overjoyed, he'd have found something else to control. In fact, Charlotte's husband controlled many areas of her life until she was finally able to leave him.

Another classic form of control is isolating you from your family and friends. This is very common in abusive relationships and is one of the reasons so many women don't realize that their mate's behaviour is not normal. If he prevents you from spending too much (or any) time with people who care about you, he is reducing the risk of you discussing his behaviour and being told how outrageous it is. Also, by cutting you off from people who like and respect you for who you are, he is making it less likely that your friendships will help you to gain strength and to improve your self-esteem, and therefore less likely that you will challenge him.

You may find that your partner wants to know exactly what you are doing for every moment of the day. If you work outside the home, he will want to know who you talked to at work, where you went for lunch, who with and so on. If you're at home taking care of the children, he may telephone several times during the day, questioning you if you're not there. When you tell him you were at the supermarket or taking the kids to school or whatever, he may quiz you about exactly how long each journey lasts and become angry if you take a few minutes longer. Charlotte again:

> I'd have to rush everywhere so that I would be back in the house when he phoned. I'd drop the kids at school but be terrified to hang around chatting with the other mums because I knew he'd phone at about 9.15, and if I wasn't there he'd be really angry. He'd accuse me of being 'out having fun' while he was slaving to pay the mortgage and feed us. One morning my son's teacher wanted to talk to me about some concerns she had about his behaviour and I didn't get home until 9.45, by which time Joe had called several times. He went absolutely berserk and even accused me of having an affair.

Having to account for every penny you spend is another controlling tactic. There is nothing wrong with normal, healthy communication between a couple who are carefully managing their finances, but when you have to give him receipts for every single thing you buy, even things for the children or personal items such as lipstick or tampons, it is neither normal nor healthy. This apparent obsession with what you spend often bears little relation to the state of your finances. Even women who are earning a good salary may have to ask their partner's 'permission' to buy something for themselves or for the house.

Sexual control may take the form of being coerced or even forced to have sex against your will, or being made to do something you're not comfortable with. Again, the coercion may be subtle so that you don't really feel justified in calling what's happening to you 'abuse'. But if your partner's standard response to a refusal in bed is anger rather than disappointment, if he frequently shouts, refuses to speak to you, accuses you of not loving him any more or of having an affair, he is being emotionally abusive.

These are general ways in which an abusive partner might try to control you, but there are many other specific examples: not allowing you to go to sleep when you're tired; not allowing you to read, watch television or talk on the telephone uninterrupted; and so on.

Wearing away your confidence and self-esteem

Many people assume that women who stay with abusive partners, women who 'allow themselves' to be abused, must be weak, timid creatures who are unable to stand up for themselves. In fact, it is often women who are strong and successful in every other area of life who find their confidence shredded by their partner. Penny is a typical example. By the age of 31, she was a senior manager in a marketing company, heading a team of twelve managers, many of them older than herself, and responsible for some of the company's most valuable accounts.

Penny

I had a reputation at work for being a bit of a 'tough cookie'. I was always fair, but I absolutely would not have any nonsense from my staff, or from the clients. I'd make middle-aged male managing directors apologize to the most junior female assistants if I thought they'd been rude. Likewise, I had no problem firing a member of staff if they deserved it. I was proud of what I'd achieved at work, and at first Ross seemed to be proud of me, too.

I met him through work and he said it was my confidence that first attracted him. But then he started making a point of belittling my achievements and putting me down in front of other people. He started picking on everything I did and said – my appearance, my cooking, my driving, even the way I spoke (I have a very slight accent). When I challenged him about it he said I was being ridiculous and paranoid. I know it sounds silly, but I actually started to believe him.

Then he said he was being critical for my own good, because he didn't want me to 'make a fool' of myself. If we had people to dinner, he'd constantly interrupt what I was saying with things like, 'Pen's got the wrong end of the stick again. What she doesn't quite understand is ...' or 'What Pen is taking a very long time to try and say is ...' But he'd smile at me as he said it as if he was just being affectionate, and so everyone would laugh indulgently as though I was a silly little woman who couldn't get to the point. Sometimes, after social occasions, he'd tell me I talked too much: didn't I notice how bored so and so was or how desperate they were to get away from me?

Consequently, I became quiet and introverted. I got to the stage where I didn't trust my own judgement any more, even about silly things like what to wear to the office. Eventually, I did become paranoid. I started to think that everybody at work was laughing at me behind my back and overriding my decisions. I became severely depressed and nearly lost my job as a result.

Fortunately, my sister who lives in Australia came over on holiday for three weeks. Ross didn't want her to stay with us, but he knew it would look odd if he refused because we were the ones with the huge house. Lynne couldn't believe the change in me. She saw what was happening almost immediately. Ross usually managed to charm people to his way of thinking, but it didn't work with Lynne, and she made me see what he was up to. In the five years we'd been together, he'd reduced me to a quivering wreck, a shadow of the woman I'd been before. With Lynne's help and that of my other sister, Jo, I managed to make the decision to leave him. It was tough at the time, but I've never looked back.

Penny's story is typical in a number of ways: her husband was attracted to her confidence and yet set out to destroy it, possibly because he felt threatened. (More on the possible explanations in Chapter 3.) He criticized Penny, humiliated her in front of friends and colleagues and then accused her of being paranoid for suggesting that his behaviour was unacceptable. Even so, he managed to convince Penny that it was only because he had her best interests at heart – i.e. he didn't want to let her 'make a fool of herself'.

By this time, Penny was so weakened by Ross's constant chipping away at her sense of self-worth that she actually believed him. Despite the fact that she'd been a hugely success-ful businesswoman who was admired and respected by her staff and colleagues, her partner had managed to convince her that she was ineffective, unattractive and socially inept. She began to question her own perceptions and doubt her own judgement.

It is not uncommon for psychologically abused women to feel they are losing their sanity as a result of this type of behaviour. In fact, some abusers seem to deliberately try to make their partners feel they are 'going mad'. This technique is sometimes known as 'gaslighting'. The term comes from the 1940s film *Gaslight*, in which a man marries a woman and then tries to drive her insane so that he can get at the jewellery she keeps locked in the attic. Gaslighting can be defined as 'a behaviour that is characterized by persistent denials of fact which, over time, have the effect of causing the victim to become anxious, confused and progressively less able to trust his or her memory of events'.

An example would be where a woman has asked her partner to pick up a loaf of bread on the way home or pay a cheque into the bank; when she asks him about it, he says, 'What are you talking about? You said you would get the bread/pay the cheque in.' No matter how much she argues, he insists that it is she who is mis-remembering their conversation. He may patronize her: 'Is it that time of the month again?' Or he may be angry or irritated with her: 'Can't I trust you to do anything?'

Women who are otherwise strong and confident, then, become less so when they feel they are 'losing the plot'. This is another way in which their partner can blame them for being 'useless' or 'incompetent', reinforcing the idea that no-one else will want them. Their partner may play on this, saying things like, 'Think yourself lucky I stay with you – no other man would put up with what I have to put up with.'

Making you think that no-one else would even put up with you, much less actually want you, is a form of emotional blackmail, another powerful tool in the abuser's armoury. Emotional blackmail may take the form of threats to leave, which can be especially effective if, for example, you have young children and are dependent on him for money. Or it may be that if you do something he doesn't like, or don't do something he wants you to do, the manner in which he shows his displeasure makes life uncomfortable or unpleasant for you or for the rest of the family. This may take the form of refusing to speak to you – 'the silent treatment' – or it may be withdrawing in other ways, such as by staying out with friends or locking himself away from the family while he's at home. In effect, he is punishing both you and your children by withholding not only his affection but his actual presence. Even if he is there physically, he may withhold communication. If you ask him what is wrong, he will probably say, 'Nothing,' in a way that makes it very clear that there *is* something wrong. Or he'll say something like, 'Well, if you don't know, I'm not going to tell you,' the implication being that you are in some way lacking: not only have you angered him, but you're too stupid to know why. The result is that you then give in to whatever it is he wants, or if you don't know what that is (and it may be just that it's the control that's important) you become extra attentive and submissive in order to improve the atmosphere or spare your children further distress.

The silent treatment can be particularly difficult to deal with, especially when you don't know what you've 'done wrong'. When you ask a sulking or silent partner what he's upset about, he is likely to reply, 'Nothing,' because that means you have no possible way of resolving it, so again he is in control of the situation. If he were to say, 'I'm feeling upset because you were busy when I came in and you didn't seem to have time for me,' you would have the opportunity to respond, perhaps by suggesting a time later in the evening when the two of you can sit down and spend some time together. So not only is he blaming you for his own feelings, he is also denying you the opportunity to address and resolve any problems. This has the effect of sapping your confidence and self-esteem even further.

While some people use silence as a weapon, others use noise: shouting, slamming doors, banging things around and listening to music, radio or television at high volume. Even in a healthy relationship, it's not unusual for one partner to enjoy very loud music to the annoyance of the other; but in a healthy relationship this can usually be resolved. It is when noise is being used *because* the other person doesn't like it that it becomes abusive behaviour. When your partner seems to be creating noise either deliberately to upset you (in retaliation for some misdemeanour you're not aware of) or with complete disregard to whether you're upset or not, you may feel intimidated or even threatened. Women who are being emotionally and psychologically abused may find that they often feel depressed and emotionally fragile. If you feel like this, having someone shouting, slamming doors and so on can make you appear nervous and 'jumpy'; he will then probably tell you that you are neurotic, and you may well start to believe him. Linda left her abusive husband over ten years ago, and she is still unable to tolerate loud or sudden noises:

Linda

Dennis seemed to swing between being silent one minute and noisy the next. Either he was sulking or he was shouting and crashing around. He slammed the door so hard once that the glass fell out, and he also broke a mug simply by banging it down on the table – we weren't having a row or anything, it was just his way of showing me he was annoyed. When he came into a room, he'd kick or punch the door open. I honestly used to think it would only be a matter of time before he started kicking and punching me.

I think the worst thing was at night. He'd always wait until I was asleep before he came to bed, then he'd hit the light switch, throw the contents of his pockets – loose change, keys, etc. – on to the dressing-table and drop his shoes on to the floor noisily. Then he'd get his clothes ready for work the next day, which meant he'd open and shut drawers really noisily as well. I asked him once if he could get his stuff ready earlier in the evening so that it was less likely to wake me up, but he went into a week-long sulk and was even noisier after that. I used to walk around like a zombie from lack of sleep and a nervous wreck due to all the noise. I never had a problem with noise before I was married; now, I'm hypersensitive to it.

By using a combination of silence and noise to abuse Linda, her husband managed to control, intimidate, threaten and punish her all at once, totally draining her of any sense of self-worth.

Verbal abuse

All couples shout at one another occasionally, possibly swearing or saying things they really don't mean. In a normal, non-abusive relationship, this is unpleasant, and it may cause a falling out lasting hours or even days. In most cases, however, one or both parties will apologize eventually and the issue will be discussed and resolved after a fashion, even if this means agreeing to disagree.

What is different about this type of behaviour in an abusive relationship is that it is a frequent rather than an unusual occurrence, and it tends to be followed by more anger and more shouting rather than apologies and attempts to resolve whatever started the argument in the first place. Indeed, what started it in the first place is often something unreasonable: for example, you didn't buy the right cheese or you spent too long on the phone to your mother.

Shouting and swearing is unpleasant and can be intimidating and very frightening, especially as it is probably coupled with other aggressive behaviour such as a furious facial expression, snarling or speaking through gritted teeth, or threatening behaviour such as shaking a fist or jabbing a finger at you. When someone behaves in this way, you may fear that the verbal abuse will become physical, and this makes you even more nervous and lacking in confidence.

Verbal abuse may be used in other ways, such as insults and name-calling. One woman (not interviewed for this book) tells how her husband constantly referred to her, in front of their children, as 'that stupid cow'. He also addressed her directly using a term too offensive to use here.

Some abusers use threats of physical violence to terrify their victim. They may threaten to hurt – even kill – you, your children, your family or your pets. Again, this is used as a form of control: 'I'll smash your face in if you don't ...'

If challenged about these threats, the abuser is likely to ridicule the suggestion that he has done anything wrong. He will say that of course he didn't mean he was really going to hurt you, and what's more it just proves what a complete idiot you are for even thinking such a thing. He may even cite an occasion when, exasperated with the kids, you said something like, 'I'll throttle you if you don't pick those toys up.' You shouldn't have said it, of course, but we all say daft things sometimes, and you said it in such a way that it didn't frighten them any more than if you'd said, 'I'll turn the telly off if you don't pick those toys up.' Less, in fact, because they don't know what 'throttle' means, and the loving care you demonstrate most of the time means they are completely secure in the certain knowledge that you won't hurt them. However, when your partner said, 'I'll smash your face in,' you were not sure that he didn't mean it, because his behaviour towards you has not been loving and caring, but aggressive and hurtful. If you argue that when you said something similar, you didn't mean it, he's likely to ridicule your attempts to point out the difference, leaving you wondering whether you are overreacting after all.

Sarcasm, verbal humiliation, ridicule and put-downs, like those experienced by Penny (see p. 8), are unpleasant and damaging, as are shouting and swearing, insults and threats. All are forms of verbal abuse and all will wear away your self-esteem and confidence, as well as making your day-to-day life miserable.

Your partner may also attack your own verbal communication. This may be by constantly interrupting you so that you cannot finish what you are saying, mimicking you in order to ridicule what you are saying, or simply ignoring the fact that you are speaking – for example, not responding verbally or not looking at you even when you speak to him directly.

This chapter has looked at a number of ways in which one person can abuse another without using physical violence. The harm caused by these types of behaviour can be as painful as that caused by physical abuse, the scars as long-lasting. And yet many women continue to put up with the abuse for years and years, often because their partner has almost total control over them and has convinced them, without necessarily setting out to do so, that they do not deserve to be treated any better.

If, having read this chapter, you are still in any doubt as to whether your partner's behaviour constitutes abuse, have a look at the following questions:

• Do you feel that your partner dominates you and controls your life?

- Does he get angry or accuse you of having an affair if you talk to someone else?
- Do you feel as though you're 'walking on eggshells', unable to do anything right?
- Does he humiliate, insult, shout at and/or swear at you?
- Does he make you account for every minute of your time? Control your money? Tell you what to wear and how to do your hair?
- Does he constantly criticize you, tell you that you're useless and stupid and couldn't cope without him?
- Does he do things because he knows they will upset you, such as locking you out of the house after an argument or driving fast because he knows it scares you?
- Does he threaten to hurt or kill you, your family or your pets?
- Does he smash up the furniture or destroy your possessions?
- Is he charming one minute, abusive the next?
- Does he try to cut you off from family and friends?
- Does he threaten to kidnap the children?

These are all examples of abuse. If you frequently experience any of these sorts of behaviours within your relationship, you need to take steps now, either to change the behaviour and repair the relationship, or to get away before your mental and physical well-being suffer any further damage. (See Chapters 4 and 5.)

2

Why is it harmful?

'Sticks and stones may break my bones but words will never hurt me': so goes the old saying. But this is far from the truth. Words, and the other types of abusive behaviour outlined in Chapter 1, can cause considerable mental and emotional pain, and can leave scars that take many years to heal.

The cycle of abuse

You might challenge abusive behaviour at first, but as it gradually whittles away at your confidence, it becomes harder to confront. As a result, the abuse worsens, your sense of self-worth is lowered further, you give up challenging the abuse altogether, and so it continues. It becomes a vicious circle, which may be impossible to break from within the relationship.

It may progress to physical abuse

Not all non-physical abuse progresses to physical violence, but physical violence is always preceded by non-physical abuse of some sort, so it's important to recognize that there is a very real physical danger. Domestic violence is far more prevalent than most people realize, probably because the perpetrators are very ordinary men and may be respected members of the community and popular in their social groups.

They often behave very differently towards their partners in public from the way they do at home. It's always difficult to acknowledge that the person you once loved – or may still love – is abusing you, whether physically or otherwise, and this, together with the respectable front their partners present to the outside world, makes it difficult for abused women to speak out. They may feel that no-one will believe them, that their partner can't help it, that they deserve it in some way or even that all men are like this and that his behaviour is normal. For this reason, the abuse remains hidden.

The following statistics give some idea of the scale of physical domestic violence:

- Two women are killed by their partners or ex-partners each week in the UK.
- The police receive around 570,000 calls a year for assistance in cases of domestic violence – that's a call every minute!
- According to the British Crime Survey, less than half of all domestic violence is reported to the police.

If your partner is physically violent, if he threatens violence or if you feel frightened by his behaviour, you might need help to manage the situation or to get yourself and your children to a place of safety. Women's Aid may be able to help – see Useful addresses, p. 105 for contact details.

Physical health

Living in an abusive relationship is bound to affect your physical health as well as your mental health. There is, as already mentioned, the very real risk of physical injury, such as broken bones, cuts, bruises and lost teeth and hair. In addition, living with emotional abuse may make you more prone to stress-related symptoms, such as insomnia, irritable bowel syndrome, headaches, high blood pressure and so on. You may lose your appetite or you may overeat, perhaps because you are drawn to unhealthy 'comfort' foods that are high in sugar and fat. The lack of a healthy diet, together with the effects of stress, can reduce the efficiency of your immune system, making you more likely to pick up infections such as colds and flu. Stress and/or depression or anxiety can also make you more likely to indulge in unhealthy behaviours such as smoking, using illegal drugs or drinking too much alcohol, which may make you feel better temporarily but can damage your health, as well as mental functions such as reasoning and decision-making.

If you are ill or physically below par, it can be difficult to cope with even the normal stresses and strains of relationships, but when you're in a relationship with someone who is abusing you, it is even more difficult to cope if you're not physically fit. It is therefore important to stay as healthy as you possibly can under the circumstances; this will give you more strength, both physically and mentally, to cope with the challenges ahead. See Chapter 4 for tips on diet, exercise and sleep.

Mental health

Abuse can, not surprisingly, lead to depression, anxiety and other mental health problems including self-harm, eating disorders and substance misuse, all of which make it even more difficult to challenge your partner's behaviour and to cope with the abuse. It may be difficult for you to seek help, especially if your partner trivializes your problems, for example, by telling you to 'stop being so miserable and cheer up' when you're actually depressed – telling someone with depression to 'cheer up' is like telling someone with a broken ankle to go for a run.

Your partner may use a diagnosis of depression as another weapon with which to abuse you, such as saying you're 'mad' or 'confused', that you can't cope without him or that you're unable to care for your children. He may threaten to have the children taken away or to have you 'locked up'. There is still a stigma attached to depression and other mental health disorders, and if your partner is telling everyone you're mentally unstable, it becomes even more difficult for you to talk to anyone about the abuse for fear that they won't believe you. See Chapter 4 for advice on recognizing and treating depression.

Relationships with family and friends

Your relationships with your friends and family can suffer as a result of your partner's behaviour, and yet these are the very relationships that you need to sustain you while you're going through this traumatic time.

As we have seen, one of the most common forms of abuse is isolating you from your family and friends. The result is that not only are the people who love you the most denied any chance of seeing what is happening to you, but they may also feel that you no longer want their love and friendship – after all, why don't you come to see them any more?

In my own case, my poor mum thought I didn't want to see her, because although I visited every week or two (she lived fairly near me) I never stayed for more than half an hour or so because I knew I'd 'get in trouble' when I got home. Before I had the children, I would occasionally go to visit a friend on my own; but as punishment my husband would withdraw from me completely for a few days afterwards, often not speaking to me at all. The same thing would happen if I talked about colleagues from work, especially if I'd dared to go for a drink with them at lunchtime (after work would have been out of the question – I needed to be home 'on time'). Gradually, I stopped seeing friends unless they were people we were both friendly with – he had no real friends of his own, and this was a warning sign I should have noted.

So with your friends and family feeling you've abandoned them, not only is there little chance of their spotting what is happening to you, there is also little chance of your observing, unimpeded, the more healthy relationships they are having and comparing those relationships with your own. Also, without the valuable love and support of your family and friends, your own self-esteem, which is being hacked away at by your partner, is not being healed by the people who value and respect you. As a result, your self-confidence suffers even more, and you become increasingly less likely to challenge the behaviour that is damaging you.

In summary, being isolated from your loved ones not only weakens the quality of your life by denying you a source of pleasure, but it also aids the abuser in his control over you by lowering your sense of self-worth. In addition, your perceptions of what is 'normal' in love, life and relationships become distorted because you no longer have anything to compare them with, nor do you trust your own judgements.

How it can affect your children

Children are damaged by divorce, we are told, and this is often true. However, children whose parents stay together can also be damaged. When children witness one parent abusing the other, there can be damage on a number of levels. First, there are the obvious ways in which children are affected. Seeing parents arguing is always upsetting for children, but the types of behaviour we're talking about here are particularly distressing, not least because the behaviour is often repeated frequently. If there is a lot of shouting and swearing, or things are being banged or thrown around, children may worry that they are going to be hurt. When they see their father being aggressive and hostile towards their mother, they may fear that she is going to be hurt. Even when children do not perceive a fear of physical harm, they will understand that their mother is extremely upset by what is happening, and even children who are too young to understand what is being said can sense fear and distress in their mother.

Older children will, of course, understand much of what is going on, and this can lead to effects that may not become apparent for many years. It can be the case, though it is by no means necessarily so, that children repeat the behaviour they've seen in their parents when they themselves are adults, in terms either of being abusive to their partners or of being abused.

It is sometimes the case that children become unwillingly involved. They may, for example, be coerced by the abuser into joining in with the verbal abuse: 'Isn't your mother a stupid cow? Isn't she? Answer me!' Even if children aren't made to join in, they are often in the room when their mother is being shouted at or humiliated. Even very young children can feel responsible for their mothers and guilty that they feel powerless to stop the abuse. This can lead to a build-up of anger that can cause problems in the future.

Men who are aggressive and abusive to their partners are often also aggressive and abusive towards their children, but when a mother is being abused in this way it can be difficult for her to protect her children. Even when it is only the mother who is the abuser's target, the children are still affected: children who witness ongoing abuse, whether it's physical or psychological, are being emotionally abused themselves. In fact, Section 120 of the Adoption and Children Act 2002 extends the legal definition of 'harm' to children to include: 'impairment suffered from seeing or hearing the ill-treatment of another'.

Children respond in many different ways and some will cope better than others, but there are a number of signs that they may be reacting badly to what's happening. For example:

- They are unusually quiet and unwilling to play.
- They have nightmares or their sleep is fitful and disturbed.
- They wet the bed.
- They become aggressive.
- They seem depressed or anxious.
- They complain of tummy aches or other aches and pains.
- They are reluctant to go to school or to leave you.

- Older children may start playing truant, smoking, drinking or using drugs. They may self-harm or develop an eating disorder, or they may run away from home.

It should be remembered, of course, that there may be other causes for all these sorts of behaviours. It should also be borne in mind that, just because a child doesn't appear to be affected by what is going on at home, it doesn't mean that he or she will not later display signs of disturbance. Children in this situation often feel frightened, bewildered, insecure, angry or guilty. They may love the abusing parent and feel divided loyalties because they want to protect the abused parent.

If you think your child is suffering as a result of your partner's behaviour, you will need support and advice to help you to help him or her. Talk to your GP in the first instance and try to be as honest as possible in explaining the situation. It's also a good idea to make your child's teachers aware of difficulties at home that may affect his or her performance at school.

Emotional and behavioural problems may continue to affect children long after the abusive relationship has ended, and indeed may only be noticed or may become worse once they are away from the situation. This is likely to be due to a combination of the trauma of the split together with the distress they've experienced as a result of the abuse.

3

Whom does it affect?

Abuse, whether physical or non-physical, can happen to anyone, regardless of social background, age, gender, religion, sexuality or ethnicity. It can happen in heterosexual and in same-sex relationships, although statistics show the vast majority of domestic violence incidents are carried out by men and experienced by women. It is fairly safe to assume that the same applies to non-physical abuse.

Why does it happen?

Abuse happens as a result of the abuser's need to establish and maintain power over his partner; he can only function if he feels 'in control', and can only feel in control by dominating her. There may be other factors involved, such as alcohol or illegal drugs, but these are not a 'cause' of the abuse.

Psychological and emotional abuse may become worse or more evident as a result of a certain trigger that threatens the abuser's sense of power – for example, when his partner lands a top job or gets promoted. It is unlikely that there will have been no evidence of abuse before the trigger event, but it may have been less noticeable. Women in this situation often say their partners show no interest in or trivialize their achievement. A controlling man's power is also threatened, of course, when his partner makes the decision to leave him, and this is another point at which abuse may become evident or may escalate (see Chapter 5).

Geraldine
When I was offered a top research position with a well-known think-tank I was thrilled, but when I told Alan, instead of congratulating me, he

sneered and made some comment about the guy who interviewed me having a thing about redheads. When I told him what salary I'd be on, he snorted with laughter and said it was unbelievable what some people would pay to have a pretty face around. The awful thing was, part of me wondered if there was some truth in what he was saying. Even though I was frequently complimented on my work – sometimes from very high levels – I still doubted my abilities because of Alan's comments. Five years on, I can't believe I was so insecure.

When I think about it now, I can see that he must have felt threatened by my achievements, because his behaviour got worse each time things went well for me.

It seems crazy, because Alan was successful in his own right; I supported him and was proud of everything he did, but it wasn't reciprocal. I was often sent abroad with my job, and when I'd return from a few days away, instead of being pleased to see me Alan would give me the silent treatment. I'd come through the door, shout, 'Hi, I'm back,' and he wouldn't even look in my direction. I'd have been looking forward to seeing him all the way back, and it was such a let-down.

I don't think I have ever cried as much in my life as I did in the three years we were together. I can't believe I stayed as long as I did!

Nikki

I was convinced Sam would be pleased for me when I told him about the project management job I'd just landed. They'd offered me the position at the end of the interview, and I wasn't expecting to know so soon, so I was really excited. I rushed home to tell Sam, but he was watching *Neighbours* and he didn't even take his eyes off the television. When I told him that I'd be expected to go abroad for a few days every few months, he said, 'You're not going.' He said it as though it wasn't up for negotiation, and he still didn't look away from the television screen! He showed no interest in anything I did, but he still thought he could dictate to me.

Abuse in pregnancy

Pregnancy is another common trigger for abuse. In fact, research shows that around 30 per cent of domestic violence starts when a woman is pregnant or shortly after the birth, and women who are in abusive relationships experience an escalation of the abuse when they become pregnant. This may be the point at which emotional and psychological abuse becomes physical. There are thought to be a number of possible explanations:

- The abusive partner sees the baby as a rival for his partner's attention.
- He feels threatened by something over which he thinks he has no control.
- He believes that the doctors and midwives his partner sees at ante-natal visits will influence her against him.
- He does not like the physical and emotional changes caused by the pregnancy.
- His partner is more vulnerable.

Emotional abuse is particularly hard to deal with in pregnancy, when you most need love, support and reassurance. It's also difficult to admit that your partner, who you expected to be misty-eyed, proud and adoring of both you and the unborn baby, is actually abusing you at this critical time. Even if the abuse doesn't become physical, it can still be damaging to the baby as well as to the mother – we now know that stress hormones can actually cross the placenta. When the abuse is physical, there is the obvious risk of injury to both mother and child; there is also a greater risk of miscarriage or stillbirth. Health care providers are now becoming alert to the problem of abuse in pregnancy and many are developing strategies to address this. Unfortunately, while most include emotional, verbal and psychological abuse in their lists of abusive behaviours, many still appear to concentrate on physical violence, thus excluding women who feel that if they're not being beaten, they have nothing to complain about.

What type of person becomes an abuser?

Emotional and psychological abusers are often people who feel inadequate, so they need to dominate their partners in order to feel important and powerful. They are often – but not always –

loners who may have lots of acquaintances but few, if any, close friends. They tend to have low self-esteem, lacking confidence in their own abilities and feeling threatened by the achievements and accomplishments of others, which explains why they belittle and trivialize anything their partner achieves.

They are often insecure and possessive: the abuser needs to 'own' his partner so that she cannot leave – if she is always there, always exactly where he wants her to be, it reassures him that he is loved, wanted and admired.

These abusers are often emotionally immature. They are unable to talk about their own feelings in an adult way so they withdraw, becoming cold, distant and unresponsive. They blame others for their problems and may 'punish' you for the way they feel, either by aggressive behaviour or by withdrawing from you emotionally and verbally. In many cases, these men have grown up in emotionally or physically abusive families.

Dr Sally Henry, a psychologist who specializes in bullying among children, suggests that bullying and controlling behaviour in adults may have the same possible cause as it often does in children: a build-up of anger and associated powerlessness, possibly going back to their own childhood. As Dr Henry says,

> Children growing up in families where there is a lot of hostility and aggression are not only likely to copy certain behaviours from their parents, they are also likely to be angry. Anger is a common emotion in children who are unhappy and do not feel secure in their home environment. They may also be angry and frustrated with themselves for being unable to solve their parents' problems – children often blame themselves for parental difficulties.
>
> This is a particular problem for boys, who, because they find it much more difficult to talk about their emotions than girls, tend to resort to maladaptive ways of coping with their feelings such as internalising or lashing out. Consequently, they can grow up in a state of rage, which manifests as abusive and controlling behaviour as they struggle to regain some power. As boys seek to understand 'what it is to be a man' so they observe strategies from father figures for obtaining this omnipotence and crucially for

boys 'daddy teaches me how to love mummy'. Sadly these ideas often also extend to female partners in the future.

Dr Henry suggests that all children experiencing family breakdown should be encouraged to discuss their feelings about their situation as a way of reducing the possibility of a build-up of anger (see the suggestions for 'special time', pp. 81–2).

Childhood experience may be a factor in the way abusive men now behave, but it is not an excuse; emotional, verbal and psychological abuse is never acceptable. We all choose the way we behave – your partner can choose not to abuse you.

The abuser often:

- feels he is always right;
- denies the abuse;
- feels his needs are more important than yours;
- is irritable, short-tempered and impatient;
- is tense, quick to anger and resentful;
- is insensitive to your feelings and opinions;
- is suspicious and paranoid;
- has frequent mood swings.

Some abusers will fit this profile very closely, while others may appear to have only a few of the traits listed here. Similarly, some abusers will demonstrate many different types of abusive behaviour, while others will display only two or three (see the list on pp. 1–2). This can make it even more difficult for the victim to recognize what is happening.

Nikki was at a very low ebb when she saw a Relate counsellor (see p. 106) in an attempt to save her marriage to Sam.

Nikki

I assumed that I was failing as a wife, because I couldn't make Sam happy. I was doing everything I could, but he had no interest in me or in our daughter. We'd been together for over ten years by the time we finally separated. He was so uninterested in me physically that I thought I must be unattractive. I was the main wage-earner – he never kept a job because he found work too stressful – but I always bought cheap clothes so that he could have the designer clothes he loved. I also paid off most of his debts, although when I expressed doubt about paying the rest, he said I was selfish and unsupportive. I paid for him to do various courses and training, none of which he completed. A couple of years ago, he decided he wanted to join the police force, but he owed almost £16k at the time, which would have gone against him, so I paid it off; but he never bothered to apply.

He'd never spend any time with me, preferring to watch television – he'd switch it on when he got up and watch it the entire time he was in the house until he went to bed. When I complained, he said it was my fault because I was doing other things – I was setting up an online business so I was often on the computer. I was very conscious of the fact that he felt he wasn't getting enough attention from me, and when our daughter was born I made sure I gave Sam plenty of attention so he didn't feel left out; it never occurred to me that he wasn't giving *me* any attention.

He criticized me all the time, but it was quite subtle at first and I just thought that I wasn't being a very good wife. I realized it was more serious than that when he refused to get out of bed when I was in labour. The midwife ended up telling him to come and support me, but all he said was, 'I don't want to get blood on my trainers.' He didn't show any affection, there was no love, no sex. I thought I must be really unattractive. Then he started accusing me of having affairs. He'd say things like, 'I know what you're up to, I know you're seeing someone else. I'm going to tell your parents the truth about you.' The worst point was when I developed an infection and he was convinced I had a sexually transmitted disease. I was so upset I told the nurse at the family planning clinic, and she called him in to explain that it was a simple infection. I felt utterly humiliated.

He put me down so often that I didn't even notice – he was always calling me 'stupid woman', 'silly cow' or 'daft bint'. It was only when our daughter, who was three at the time, started saying the same things that I realized it wasn't normal. I was desperately unhappy, but I still didn't see what Sam was doing as wrong. I suggested relationship counselling, but Sam refused to come – he said it was my problem. It was the Relate counsellor who showed me that although Sam wasn't physically hurting me, he was abusing me. It was that realization that enabled me to grow stronger and to challenge his behaviour. I made it clear that I wouldn't put up with it any more and Sam made it clear that he was not going to change. When he said he wanted a divorce, I said 'fine', and saw my solicitor the next day. Sam was horrified – he thought I'd beg and plead with him, but it's too late now, and we're currently going through a divorce. He says he doesn't want this, but at the same time he's telling me I'm 'not right in the head', that I 'need help' and that I'm 'an unfit mother'.

Now I'm away from him, I find that I'm highly valued at work and am good at my job. I used to think I wasn't earning a good salary, but that was because I was always clearing Sam's debts or paying for him to do some course or other, none of which he ever completed. I realize now that I'm not the selfish, useless, ugly person he said I was. I've realized that I am attractive after all, that the things I do aren't all stupid, and that I do deserve some love and affection.

Nikki put her husband first again and again, but he still wasn't happy, so she blamed herself. Sam reinforced the idea that Nikki was to blame by making her feel guilty for not making his life perfect. He then threatened her with divorce out of his own insecurity – he'd expected her to make him feel important by begging him to stay, and was astonished when she agreed to the divorce with some degree of relief.

What type of person falls prey to abuse?

People who have not experienced abuse cannot understand how women can allow themselves to be treated like this, so they assume that the women concerned must be weak in some way, or must enjoy being a doormat. This is not the case. As we have already seen, this type of abuse is often insidious and hard to recognize, even when it's happening to you. Women who are being abused often think they are simply attempting to be good wives and partners, endeavouring to support their partner and make his life easier, and trying to avoid doing the things that make him uncomfortable. On the surface, there is nothing wrong with this – it is natural to want to make things easier for the person you love. But a healthy relationship is one in which this works both ways, and as in Nikki's case (see above) it is often the case that the abuser puts his own desires way above those of his partner, who may strive to satisfy them without ever addressing her own needs.

So why don't we recognize this type of behaviour when it starts? And why do we not avoid relationships with men who show themselves to be abusive even in the early stages of the relationship? There are a number of reasons why some women not only fail to run for the hills when they experience this behaviour, but may even be attracted to men who become abusive. These include:

- poor role models – seeing your mother or other female relatives being abused by their partners;
- being used to being treated badly;
- having low self-esteem and therefore low expectations of relationships.

Poor role models

We learn by example. If your mother tiptoed around your father, blamed herself for making him angry and said, 'Sorry,' when he swore at her for overcooking the cabbage, if she made excuses for his lack of support and was grateful that he chose to stay with such a useless, stupid and unattractive woman as herself, it's very possible that, on some deeply buried level, you will do the same.

Maggie
When I told my mum that Dennis and I were getting married, she wasn't happy – she said he was just like my father, who'd died a couple of years before but had treated my mum very badly. I laughed. I said he was nothing like my dad. My dad used to hit my mum, and I knew Dennis would never hit me – he thought what my dad had done was terrible. But it wasn't until after I left him that I realized there were similarities, not only in how Dennis and my dad behaved, but in how my mum and I responded. Dennis didn't ever hit me but, like my dad, he had no friends and relied on me for everything. He was very possessive and controlling, and would get angry with me if things weren't exactly how he thought they should be. My dad was the same, but whereas he'd

belt my mum around the face, Dennis would just shout a lot and call me a lazy fat cow.

I did just what my mum did: instead of telling him to stop behaving badly, I fussed around all the time, apologizing for everything and trying to make sure there was nothing that could displease him. Because he didn't actually hit me, I couldn't see that he was being abusive. We were together for six years, but I never really felt loved.

Being used to poor treatment

If you grow up in a family where you are used to being beaten, shouted at, neglected, ignored, undervalued or treated without respect, you will be so used to such treatment that it will not occur to you to try to change it when you encounter it in future relationships; you may even regard it as normal. Conversely, women who grow up in families where they are treated with respect, kindness, affection and consideration will expect to be treated in the same way by their partners, and they will usually reject people who treat them differently.

Low self-esteem and low expectations

If you have low self-esteem, you may be more likely to find yourself in an abusive relationship. If you've been starved of affection and attention, you are probably more likely to make a grab for any that is offered, feeling grateful for it rather than demanding a certain amount of respect and consideration from your partner. Low self-esteem, whether it is a result of how you were treated in childhood or whether it comes from poor treatment in adult relationships, tends to lower your expectations. You may accept being treated badly because you feel – probably because you've been told – that you don't deserve to be treated any better. You may feel, as Maggie did (pp. 32–3), that you should be grateful that your partner doesn't hit you. You will probably say things like, 'Every relationship has its troubles,' 'No-one's perfect,' or 'Love isn't a bed of roses.' All true, but when your relationship gives you

more pain than pleasure, it's time to look at what is really
going on:

- Every relationship has its troubles – but in most cases,
  both partners will acknowledge some responsibility and will,
  before things get out of hand, make some effort to address the
  difficulties.
- No-one's perfect – but most people can recognize their imper-
  fections to some degree, and are at least prepared to apologize
  when something they do causes their partner distress. In a
  relationship between two people, each will upset or anger the
  other occasionally, but in healthy relationships there will be
  a fairly equal balance. If one person is constantly angry and
  the other constantly distressed, something is not right.
- Love isn't a bed of roses – but nor should it be a pit of thorns!

4

What can you do?

In some cases, the only realistic course of action is to end the relationship: for example, if your partner is physically violent or threatens you with violence, if your children are being directly abused or are suffering as a result of what is happening to you, or if you're fairly certain that things won't change. Chapter 5 looks in more detail at how you might make the decision to end the relationship and what might be involved, including practical advice, if you do. This chapter, however, will concentrate on what you can do from within the relationship if you feel there is a realistic chance of it surviving. Whatever you decide to do, your safety and that of your children is paramount, and it cannot be stressed highly enough that you should not take any action (from within the relationship) that you feel may trigger physical violence.

Staying safe

Even if your partner has never hurt you physically, you cannot be entirely certain that the abuse will not become physical at some point. As we have seen, not all emotional abuse becomes physical, but all physical abuse begins with emotional abuse, so you need to make sure that you and your children stay as safe as possible while you continue to live with your partner. The following safety tips may be useful:

- Keep your mobile phone charged and with you at all times. It may be an idea to set up speed-dialling, and possibly to have an emergency text message in your outbox, ready to send.

If you don't have a mobile, make sure you know where the nearest phone is, should you need to call the police.

- Teach your children how to dial 999 and give their name, address and telephone number.
- Think about having a code word or phrase that you can use to alert friends or family that you're in trouble.
- If you know and trust your neighbours, ask them to call the police if they hear an attack.
- If you suspect your partner is about to hurt you, try to stay in areas of the house where you can get out quickly if you need to. Avoid rooms where he could lock you in, and try to make sure potential 'weapons' are kept out of sight – for example, kitchen knives, heavy objects, hot irons, etc.
- Keep a little money on you all the time in case you find yourself running away from him and needing to pay fares or make phone calls.
- Have a spare set of car keys cut, and keep an emergency bag packed. Hide these safely in the house or in the house of someone you can trust (see pp. 52–3 for what to pack).

Changing behaviour patterns

In order to repair a relationship damaged by abuse, the behaviour of both partners will need to change significantly. As a victim of abuse, you need to take a stand against your partner, to tell him and show him that you will not take the sole blame for problems in the relationship, that the responsibility for his abusive behaviour is his and his alone, and that you are not prepared to put up with that behaviour. You cannot, however, change his behaviour for him – he is the only one who can do that.

Will he ever change?

Getting the abuser to change is difficult, mainly because most abusers are not prepared even to consider that there is anything wrong in the way they treat their partners. The abuser often believes his partner is to blame and so he heaps responsibility for his own behaviour on to her: 'Why do you keep making me lose my temper?' In order for your partner to change his behaviour, he needs to accept that it has been abusive, and he needs to be willing to make a commitment to change.

The first step, provided you are sure it is safe to do so, is to confront him. Before doing so, you should be fairly sure that there is at least a reasonable chance that he will be responsive. You are the only person who can make a judgement as to whether you should confront him about his behaviour and, indeed, whether you can do so safely. He will not like what you are saying, but it may be that he is prepared to consider it. If you feel that confronting him would make things worse, it may be better to think about ending the relationship rather than trying to change it.

If you do decide to confront your partner, you may want to choose a time when things are reasonably calm. This can be difficult, because when you're used to living in a very volatile atmosphere, there's a temptation to avoid doing anything that might threaten periods of calm. The alternative is to confront him at the time, which may be a good option if you suspect he is genuinely unaware that his behaviour is abusive.

Hopefully, reading this book will have helped you to clarify the situation so that you are able to pinpoint the abusive nature of his comments or actions, which will be helpful if you decide to confront him at the time. You may also find these suggestions useful:

- When he says or does something you find abusive, tell him as calmly and sensitively as you can what he has done to offend or upset you, but do not apologize for your feelings by starting your sentences with, 'I'm sorry, but ...'
- Be direct and firm, assertive but not aggressive.
- Use 'I' statements rather than 'you' statements: for example,

'I find that language upsetting and offensive, and I'd be grateful if you wouldn't use it when we're talking to each other,' rather than, 'You're always swearing at me.'

- As well as telling him what isn't acceptable, tell him how you wish to be treated: for example: 'If you're unhappy with the way I've done something, would you please tell me about it when we're alone rather than in front of our friends.'
- Avoid words like 'always' and 'never': 'You're always criticizing,' or 'You never phone when you're going to be late.'
- On no account should you confront your partner if you suspect he might hurt you or your children as a result.

The same advice also applies if you decide to choose a quiet time to talk to him about his behaviour. In addition, you may find these suggestions helpful:

- You could start the conversation by saying something like, 'I'm sure you've noticed that things have been a bit difficult between us recently, and I'd like the two of us to discuss it together.'
- When you address the behaviour, you could say: 'I know you probably don't mean to hurt or upset me, but I do feel hurt and upset when you …'
- You may also want to show him that you understand why he behaves the way he does: 'I know you were badly treated by your father/mother/carer, and it may be why this behaviour seems normal to you …'
- Allow him to respond and listen to what he says (as long as he doesn't become abusive, in which case this probably isn't going to work). Try to understand his feelings and intentions, and ask him to try to understand yours.
- Don't bring up too much in one go, because he'll probably become defensive and it'll be impossible to continue a sensible discussion.

- If either of you find yourselves becoming angry or defensive, take a break and agree to resume the discussion later.
- Suggest you attend relationship counselling together.
- Suggest he attends a men's group or perpetrators programme, such as those promoted by the organization Respect (see Useful addresses, p. 104).

It will probably be clear to you fairly quickly whether these approaches are likely to be productive. If your partner becomes aggressive, refuses to listen, ridicules your feelings, denies the abuse and refuses to seek help or attend counselling, you may have to accept that nothing is going to change.

Changing your own behaviour

No-one deserves to be abused, and all types of abuse are *always* the responsibility of the abuser. However, if you continue to accept being treated poorly without challenging the behaviour, the abuser is likely to take your silence as compliance and use it as an invitation to continue abusing you. Having said that, we have already seen just how difficult it can be to challenge abusive behaviour when you are emotionally and physically weakened by what you have already experienced.

If you have confronted him and found him willing to at least attempt to change, you have something to build on. From now on, you must make it clear that you will not tolerate his abusive behaviour. This may mean using assertive phrases like, 'I find that unacceptable' or 'I'm not prepared to do that.' You may already feel stronger for having confronted him, but in order to maintain that strength, you need to concentrate on looking after yourself and regaining control of your life.

Becoming more assertive

Many women, and particularly those in abusive relationships, are bad at putting their needs before those of other people. It is likely that you have been conditioned, possibly by your role models but almost certainly by your abusive partner, to believe that your needs are not as important as his and that to ask for what you want is a selfish act. If your partner blames you for his behaviour, you may subconsciously be ignoring your own needs in order to make up for what you see as your 'failings' and under the mistaken impression that you will be liked and valued more if you put yourself last.

Learning to be assertive is difficult for many women, but it will help you to regain control of your life by accepting that you have the same rights as other people and that you deserve to be valued and respected.

Being assertive is not about being aggressive, but about valuing all opinions – including your own. It is about being able to communicate effectively with everyone you meet in daily life, being able to say 'no' when you don't want to do something, and being able to set boundaries and enforce them. For example: 'I will not allow anyone to hurt me or abuse me sexually,' 'I will not allow anyone to use offensive language when talking to me,' or 'I will not allow illegal drugs/stolen goods/pornography in my home.'

Try to be aware of your body language when communicating. Are your shoulders hunched? Do you avoid eye contact? If so, you are adopting a classic 'victim' stance. Try standing upright, in a relaxed manner and maintaining calm, friendly eye contact with the person you're talking to. Practise in the mirror if necessary. State your message calmly, clearly and directly. If the other person tries to change the subject, point this out and repeat the message. If the other person argues, listen to their point of view and offer a compromise if possible, but don't give up your own view – a compromise involves sacrifice on both sides.

If you possibly can, sign up for an assertiveness training course – your local library should have details of classes and most adult education institutes offer assertiveness training courses, many of which are specifically for women.

Becoming and staying healthy

As we have already seen, coping with an abusive relationship can adversely affect your physical and mental health, so it's important to address this. Whatever you decide to do about your situation, dealing with it is going to be a huge drain on your energy stores – that's if you have any energy left! Taking care of your health as far as possible can help you become stronger and more able to face the battle ahead. A few simple steps you can take are:

Eat a healthy diet

A healthy diet can boost your immune system and reduce your risk of serious illness such as heart disease and diabetes. Try to eat at least two pieces of fruit and three portions of vegetables each day and adopt the 'rainbow' approach – choose fruit and veg in a variety of colours to get the best mix of vitamins and other nutrients. Cut down on salt, processed foods, foods that are high in fat, and sugary things like sweets, cakes and biscuits. Eat two portions of oily fish each week and eat plenty of pulses, seeds and wholegrains.

Take enough exercise

You don't have to join a gym, just make sure you take a brisk 20-minute walk at least four times a week. Not only does exercise help you to lose weight or maintain a healthy weight, it also tones muscles, helps you to sleep and stimulates your brain to release chemicals called endorphins, which help lift your mood – very important if you're living in a situation that is making you increasingly unhappy.

Get enough sleep

This can be difficult when you're unhappy and worried sick about what's going to happen, but there are things you can do to make sleep more likely:

- Avoid heavy meals too close to bedtime, and avoid caffeine, alcohol and nicotine.
- Keep your bedroom as dark and quiet as possible, and sleep in a slightly cool room, preferably with the window open.
- A few drops of lavender oil in a warm bath and on your pillow can help.
- Try a valerian-based natural remedy such as Sedonium.
- If you still can't sleep, talk to your doctor.

Maintain a social life

Your friends, like your family, are your support network, as well as being fun to be with, and it's important to maintain contact with them, especially when you're going through a difficult time. Seeing your friends gives you a chance to relax, to think about something other than your relationship, and to laugh! Laughing is a great stress reliever and even smiling is good for depression – research suggests that using the facial muscles associated with smiling triggers the release of certain chemicals in the brain that help lift mood.

Friends and family can also provide a sense of normality that may be missing from your life with your partner; when he's telling you you're stupid and useless, those who love you will show how much they value you. When he tells you you're going mad, your friends and family will confirm that there's nothing wrong with your perceptions. In many cases, it's friends or family members who can see what's happening before you are really ready to accept it.

As already mentioned, in my own case my husband tried to isolate me by sulking whenever I saw my friends and becoming angry if I spent too long visiting my family. The result was that I stopped seeing many of my friends and paid only brief visits to my family. Fortunately, I made two very good friends who were also neighbours and whose children went to school with mine, so he couldn't cut me off entirely. Those two friends were my major source of support before, and to a large degree after, I left him. They confirmed that I was sane and normal. Also, living so near, they often saw or heard his abusive behaviour.

No matter what your domestic commitments, it is always reasonable to maintain contact with friends and family; if your partner tries to prevent you from doing so, you need to ask yourself why.

Depression

Depression is a serious, potentially life-threatening illness. It can be difficult to recognize, especially in yourself. It is often a friend or family member who first notices when someone is depressed, but if your partner has cut you off from family and friends your depression is less likely to be picked up. It is even more difficult to recognize in yourself when you're living in a traumatic or distressing situation.

How to recognize depression

Depression is more than feeling 'a bit down'; if you feel very sad, bleak or hopeless for longer than a few days, you may have depression. The manifestation of the illness varies from person to person, but these are some of the signs to look out for:

- persistent low mood, often worse in the mornings;
- tearfulness;
- feeling unable to experience pleasure or enjoyment;
- loss of interest in social and work activities;
- reduced or increased appetite;
- sleep difficulties – insomnia or early wakening, or needing unusually large amounts of sleep;
- lack of energy, fatigue;
- slowed thinking, speech and/or movements;
- inability to concentrate;
- anxiety, panic attacks;

- feeling worthless and hopeless;
- being able to see only the negative side of things;
- suicidal thoughts.

You don't need to experience all of these symptoms to be suffering from depression, but depression is a serious illness that requires treatment, possibly with medication, counselling, cognitive behaviour therapy or a combination of these. Self-help books may also be useful. If you think you may be depressed, talk to your doctor about treatment. Depression and/or anxiety may be a normal reaction to the difficult circumstances you are currently in, but this does not mean it will go away by itself. It can be successfully treated in the majority of cases, although it may take several months or even a year or more. If you're treated with antidepressants, it's important to continue taking them for at least six months after you last had symptoms, and to reduce the dose gradually rather than just stopping. Don't be afraid of taking antidepressants – for the vast majority of people they are very effective and safe to use, as long as you follow your doctor or pharmacist's instructions.

While your depression can probably be treated, the under-lying cause will, of course, remain. But getting help for your depression should help you to think more clearly and to cope better with the problems you are experiencing. You may feel more able to do something about the situation, whether that involves tackling your partner's behaviour on your own, getting professional help in the form of relationship or personal counselling, or actually leaving the relationship.

Note: Some herbal preparations are very useful for mild to moderate depression, but if you are taking any other medication, check with your doctor or pharmacist before taking them. St John's Wort, for example, is an effective and gentle treatment for depression, but it may affect the action of other drugs, including the contraceptive pill.

5

The decision to leave

Many people find it difficult to understand why women stay with abusive partners, sometimes for decades. 'If it's that bad,' they say, 'why doesn't she just leave?' Or even, 'She must enjoy it, or she'd leave.' In fact, making the decision to leave an abusive relationship, especially if you have children, is extremely difficult for a number of reasons.

First, as we have already seen, there is a long period during which the abused woman tries to put things right. Her partner is likely to have convinced her that she is at fault in the relationship and that if only she were not so stupid, lazy, incompetent, needy, selfish, neurotic and paranoid (or whatever else he's told her) then things would be better. But as we have seen, the abused woman cannot improve the relationship by changing her behaviour in these ways, because there is nothing wrong with her behaviour in the first place. Again and again, the abused women quoted in this book tried to do and be what their partners wanted, but it was never enough. It never would be enough, because at the root of the abuse is the need to control, and, as in Charlotte's case (see p. 5), as soon as the abused woman satisfies one of her partner's demands, there will be another. So the first stage in ending the relationship is to accept that you will never be able to do enough to please your partner, because it is not simply that his demands are unreasonable, it is that they are endless.

Second, even if you accept that you will never be able to please your partner, it is more difficult to admit, both to yourself and to others, that you are being abused. Even when a non-abusive long-term relationship breaks up, there is often a period of denial, probably due to a combination of factors such as:

- feeling that you have 'failed' at the relationship;
- hanging on to the hope that things will improve;
- avoidance of the difficulties that ending the relationship will bring (acrimony, divorce, financial difficulties, children's distress, etc., etc.).

Towards the end of an abusive relationship, you will be affected by all these factors and more; you will have to face the fact that the man to whom you have given your love, trust and respect has denied you those things in return. You will also have to face the fact that when (and if) you tell him you are leaving because of his abuse, he will almost certainly deny it and try to blame you for the relationship problems. If your partner is one of those who is charming in the company of other people and only abuses you in private, you may have to face disbelief from those who know you as a couple. You may also be afraid of how he will react when you tell him you are going, not to mention the sheer practical difficulties of leaving home, possibly with children or pets, and finding somewhere else to stay.

All in all, then, making the decision to go is a tough one. But unless you have a very clear admission from your partner that his behaviour is abusive *and* a genuine commitment to address this, probably through counselling or a perpetrators' group (see p. 39), leaving him might, realistically, be your only option. Abusive behaviour will not just stop. In fact, it is likely to worsen over time, as it did for the women – all of them, without exception – who were interviewed for this book. In some cases, the abuse will escalate into physical violence.

The following questions may help to make your decision easier:

- Has your partner abused you physically or threatened to abuse you physically?
- Even if he hasn't threatened you, are you afraid that he might become violent?
- Have you become, or are you afraid you might become, physically violent yourself?
- Have you begun to question your sanity?
- Does he make you feel inferior to him, or as though you have no value?
- Have you found yourself fantasizing about harming or even killing him?
- Is he abusing your children, either directly or indirectly? For example, do they witness him abusing you? Do they see or hear you crying? Are they suffering as a result of your unhappiness?

If your answer to any of these questions is yes, then you should consider leaving.

Planning to go

Some women end up leaving their relationships with no prior planning, perhaps during or after a big argument or because they fear for their own or their children's safety (see 'Staying safe' on pp. 35–6). But whether or not you have been through the stages of peacemaking, denial and acceptance, if you think there is even the slightest chance you will have to leave, advance planning is recommended. Simply making plans will not commit you to anything, but you'll be able to think more clearly and make decisions more easily when you're not in the middle of an abusive episode, and some prior planning could make life easier and safer if you do need to go. Choosing to stay in an abusive relationship is certainly a risk to your emotional and physical well-being, but it would be disingenuous to pretend that leaving it will immediately remove that risk. In fact, according to Women's Aid, the period during which a woman is planning and making her exit is often the most dangerous time: her partner senses she is taking charge of her life, this threatens his control over her and the abuse worsens as he struggles to maintain his power. Safety is, therefore, crucial and you should take this into account at every stage.

The rest of this chapter will address some of the issues involved in leaving a relationship, and may help to remove at least some of the concerns you will inevitably have about taking this step.

Keeping a diary

If you consider it safe to do so, keeping a diary of the abuse can be a good idea, particularly if you're married and need to divorce your husband on the grounds of his unreasonable behaviour. A diary is a useful reminder about specific incidents – there are often so many that it's hard to remember each one – and could be used as evidence if need be. Keep a record of every incident, no matter how small – remember, calling you a silly cow once is unpleasant, but not abuse; frequent insults, criticisms and put-downs are. Record the date, time and how long the incident lasted. Make a note of exactly what he said or did, what precipitated the abuse, what you said or did in response and how you felt (crying, shaking, frightened, sick, wanted to run away).

Note: keeping a record of the abuse can be helpful, but could also be risky if your partner were to discover its existence. If you do decide to keep one, you will need to make sure he cannot find it. Possible options are:

- a written record hidden at home, in the house or outside it – only safe if you're sure he won't find it;
- a written record kept at somebody else's home – safer, but not as accessible for you, so there may be problems keeping it up to date; you could ask a friend or whoever keeps it for

you to make a brief note until you can write a fuller account
yourself;

- a computer record – again, only if you're certain he can't get
  into your documents;
- email – if there is a friend or relative you are sure you can
  trust, email them the details of the abuse. The record can
  then be printed out at a later date. Use an email programme
  that does not automatically keep a 'sent' file.

Practical preparation

It may be a good idea to start putting aside a little money each
week, preferably in a separate bank account, to help make
things easier in the first few days and weeks after you leave.
Your partner may refuse to let you back into the house to collect
clothes, toys and personal items. Many men also refuse to pay
maintenance for the children, even after a court has ordered
them to do so. This is simply another form of control, and may
be based on his belief that, if he denies you money to buy the
things you need and access to the things you already own, you
will have to come back to him. Even if you have a separate
income, there may be expenses and difficulties you hadn't antic-
ipated; if you can save a little money in preparation, it might
prove useful if something crops up.

It may be an idea to have an emergency bag packed and ready
in case you need to leave very suddenly. This should contain
spare clothes, important documents, cash, credit cards, etc. (See
'What to take with you', pp. 52–3.)

Where can you go?

Much depends on how much preparation you can do beforehand and how suddenly you have to leave. For many
women the first choice is their parents or other close

relatives. Of course, this may not be an option because of lack of room or other circumstances, but it may be worth considering as a temporary arrangement. There may be a relative to whom you can go for a few nights, or you may be able to stay for several weeks or months. If you have not told your family about your situation, you should consider doing so if you are thinking of leaving. Your family can be a tremendous source of emotional and practical help. But they will only be able to be so if they know how serious things have become. Many women put such a 'brave face' on it that their friends and family have no idea how bad the situation has become – this is especially the case if your partner has isolated you from those who care about you.

In my own case, my family knew there were problems in my marriage, but I hadn't told them just how bad things were. My sister noticed that I was, as she puts it, 'on the edge', and unbeknown to me, she, my mother and my brother-in-law (who all shared a house) held a family conference and agreed that room would be made for the children and me should we ever need to leave. When they told me this, I wept with relief. A room was cleared, a camp bed moved in and second-hand bunk beds hastily bought and put together. I moved in three days later. If I had asked for shelter beforehand I would have been given it, but it never occurred to me to ask. Nor did I consider going to a women's refuge, because I thought these were only for women who had been physically battered.

Women's Aid and Refuge jointly run the Domestic Violence National Helpline for women in crisis (see Useful addresses, p. 106), and many of the calls to the helpline are from women suffering non-physical abuse. Helpline staff will try to find you a place in one of their many safe houses across the country, and if no places are available they'll do their utmost to find you somewhere to stay, whether or not you feel you are in physical danger. They will also answer any questions you may have about going to a refuge.

You may also be entitled to emergency housing through the local authority under the Housing Act. Even if you own your home, you are considered to be legally homeless if it 'would not be reasonable' for you to occupy it: for example, when there is a risk or threat of domestic violence. In cases like this, the local authority (or housing executive in Northern Ireland) has a duty to provide 'interim accommodation' – usually a bed and breakfast hotel – while it decides whether you are legally homeless. The housing authority will normally only consider you to be in priority need if there is actual physical violence or a threat of violence, although they will consider each case on its merits as to what constitutes 'violence' for housing purposes. For example, forced sex is classed as violence, but verbal abuse, unless it contains threats of violence, is not. Menacing behaviour, such as pushing, shoving or raising his fists, may well count as a threat of violence. The housing office will not necessarily need 'proof', but anything that can support your case, such as a letter from the police or a doctor or social worker, would help.

It may in some cases be possible for the court to grant an injunction ordering your partner to vacate the family home so that you and the children can stay or, if you have left because of violence or the threat or fear of it, so that you can return. This type of injunction is known as an 'occupation order'. It can exclude your partner from the family home and the surrounding area if you can prove that there is a significant risk of harm to you or the children. It should be borne in mind that court injunctions don't always work and may even inflame the situation, so you'll need to think carefully and to get professional legal advice before taking this step. Make an appointment to see a solicitor to discuss your options (see 'Seeing a solicitor', p. 70).

Going to a refuge

A refuge is a safe house where any woman escaping physical or emotional abuse can go, with or without children. It is temporary accommodation, but you can stay as long as you need to, whether it's just for a few days or for several months while you wait for permanent accommodation. Refuge addresses are confidential, and no men are allowed in the houses.

Staff at the refuge can offer practical help in a number of areas, including:

- finding suitable permanent accommodation;
- finding a new school for your children if necessary;
- claiming benefits;
- accessing health services;
- accessing legal advice, and accompanying you to solicitors' appointments or to court;
- training, education and finding a job.

As well as offering practical help, refuge staff will understand what you've been through and will also offer emotional support, although you may find the most useful support comes from other women staying at the refuge, who will have had similar experiences to yours.

What to take with you

Try to take the following things with you when you leave – don't rely on being able to get back into your home to collect things you leave behind:

- important telephone numbers, including that of your nearest Women's Aid, refuge or other domestic violence organization;

- your diary or journal if you've kept one, especially if you've kept a record of the abuse;
- any other documents relating to the abuse: for example, any letters or reports from the police or victim support, taped telephone messages, any records of physical abuse, such as photographs or medical reports, and any legal documents, such as court injunctions or restraining orders;
- birth certificates and passports for you and the children;
- favourite toys, books and so on – you don't need to take a lot, but a few of the things that will help make your children feel more at home wherever you're going; children have a strong awareness of their surroundings, and having a few familiar things will help them to feel more settled and secure;
- clothing for you and the children, bearing in mind that the weather can change very suddenly – you may leave in summer clothing only to find that, by the following week, you need jumpers and coats; however, if you need to pack and get out quickly, just take a few basics – you can always buy cheap stuff from the charity shop to tide you over;
- cash, credit/debit cards, cheque, building society or post office books;
- benefit payment cards or books, including child benefit;
- National Insurance and NHS numbers;
- car and house keys.

Should you tell him you're going?

As already mentioned, the point at which you leave can be a dangerous time, so you need to carefully weigh up the options before deciding whether to tell him in advance. Whatever happens, it's going to be difficult and he will be angry. If you are sure that he won't attack you and you think that leaving without telling him would enrage him more, you may decide it's better to tell him before you go. If you tell him too far in advance, he may take steps to prevent you from going or to make life difficult for you if you do: for example, he may take your car keys or freeze your joint bank account. If you do tell him, do so just before you leave, and if possible arrange for someone to collect you at a definite time, so that you can tell him you're going and that someone will be there to pick you up within a few minutes. Or you can wait until the person is actually outside, then tell him and leave immediately afterwards. Have whatever you need to take with you packed and ready to go, and be prepared for his reaction, which could be anything from disbelief or outrage to tears, pleading and promises to change.

If you think that telling him you're leaving might trigger an outburst that puts you or the children at risk in any way, then don't. Arrange to leave when you know he won't be around. If he's around most of the time, or if you're worried that he may have guessed that you're planning to leave and he keeps popping home unexpectedly, you may be able to get a police escort to make sure you can get away safely.

Telling the children

No matter how young your children are, they will be aware of your unhappiness, if not of the actual abuse. It may be best not to tell the children before you leave because you would have to warn them not to tell your partner. Apart from the fact that they may well let it slip, it is not really fair to burden them, even if they're adolescents, with the responsibility of such a weighty secret. When it's time to actually go, however, it is best to tell them the truth, without going into too much detail in the case of younger children. For example, 'Daddy is treating me very badly and he won't stop, so we need to go and live somewhere else.'

Depending on whether it is considered safe, it may be that

your partner maintains contact with the children, in which case you can tell them that they'll still see their daddy even though they won't be living in the same house. If your partner has been or is likely to become physically violent, the chances are that you will not want him to know where you are going, but it may still be possible for him and the children to maintain a relationship by arranging supervised contact at a contact centre (see p. 69).

If you know where you will be staying, you can tell them this as well: 'We're going to stay at Grandma's house.' Initially, they'll probably see the whole thing as a bit of an adventure, but it will be unsettling for them, even if they've been distressed by the abuse they've witnessed. If they are very upset, it can be tempting to pretend that you're only going to be away for a few days, but you should resist this temptation. If you tell them you're having a little holiday or something similar, they'll take longer to settle into their new life because they'll be expecting to go home any day. Chapter 6 looks further at how they, and you, might feel after you've left.

What about your pets?

Pets can be important members of your family and are often a source of great comfort, especially when things are difficult. Women often say pets are a big consideration when ending their relationships, and many women continue to endure quite violent abuse rather than deprive their children of a beloved pet. Some men threaten to harm or kill pets if their partners leave, thus maintaining power and control. Some actually carry out their threats. If you have been able to arrange permanent accommodation in advance, or are going to stay with helpful and generous pet-friendly relatives, you may be able to take your pets with you, or there may be someone who will look after them for you until you are settled. If this isn't possible, there are a number of organizations, such as Paws for Kids (see p. 105), who may be able to help if you have to go to a refuge or other emergency accommodation. These organizations can sometimes place your pets in foster homes for a few months until you are able to have them with you again. Most of these organizations require some sort of 'proof' that you are fleeing an abusive relationship – this may be in the form of a letter from a refuge worker, social worker, GP or the police. Some services are free; others require a contribution to food costs and veterinary bills.

Alternatively, you may decide the best option is to have your pets re-homed, in which case you should contact a re-homing organization such as the Blue Cross (see Useful addresses, p. 105). Your local vet will be able to advise you, and may even know of someone looking for a pet.

6

After the break-up

How you might feel

Leaving a long-term relationship, even one that is abusive, is a traumatic experience for you and your children. The very fact that you have decided to leave means the abuse has become unbearable, and it is likely that you will be physically, mentally and emotionally drained by the time you actually leave. In addition, you will be worried about the future, about how you're going to cope financially, about whether your partner is going to punish you for leaving and, of course, how you are going to minimize the impact on your children. It is also possible that you will be wondering if you've done the right thing, especially as your partner, if you have contact with him, will almost certainly be telling you that you are overreacting, being neurotic, stupid, etc., etc.

You may feel lonely and isolated, especially if your partner has cut you off from your relationships with your friends and family, or if you've moved to a new area. In the early days of your separation, you may even miss your partner, perhaps feeling that putting up with an abusive partner is better than having no partner at all. This is not unusual, and it doesn't mean that you were wrong to leave. It will take a while to build new friendships, but it will happen. In the meantime, could you re-establish contact with those friends or relatives you've been cut off from? It may be worth giving them a call and explaining your situation – you may find a lot of people have some idea anyway and will understand why you've not been in touch. Chapter 7 looks at other ways of rebuilding your life.

Feeling guilty

Many women experience feelings of guilt in the early stages of a relationship break-up, especially when the children are clearly distressed by the situation. Even when the children have witnessed or experienced the abuse themselves, and even if they have seemed keen to get away, they may now be asking to go home and see Daddy. It is very difficult to comfort a distressed and traumatized child when you yourself are distressed and traumatized, and you will probably feel guilty for causing them distress. This is a normal but unhelpful response. If you had stayed in the relationship and your children had suffered as a result (as they undoubtedly would have) you would have felt guilty about that, too. Guilt is a condition of motherhood, so you'll suffer from it whatever happens; it's just that you'll feel it more keenly when faced with a crying child. Try to comfort them if you can, and remind yourself what you are escaping from and that you didn't take this decision lightly.

It's at this stage that you must be careful not to take the easy option and tell the kids that you will be going home soon, though you can reassure them that they will be able to see their father soon – if indeed that is the case. Friends and family can be a tremendous source of help and support to both you and your children at this time, and if you are staying in a women's refuge you will find the other women and the staff supportive as well.

Sadness and grief

Even when you've been treated appallingly for years, it is quite normal to feel some sadness after leaving your relationship. This may be because you still have feelings for your partner, or at least for the memory of the man you fell in love with. There is also a certain amount of grief at the loss of the relationship itself, a relationship that you will have worked at, invested in, defended and tried to preserve despite your unhappiness, possibly for many years. Even your happy memories have been soured by more recent events.

By leaving the relationship, you are acknowledging the loss of hope that things will improve; this in itself can be quite difficult to come to terms with, especially as hope may have been the only thing that has kept you going for some time. Leaving your home can also be a significant emotional wrench. Your home represents the hopes and dreams you shared with your partner in happier times, and as a nest-builder you will have invested both time and money in making an attractive and comfortable home for your family. It may be the house you came to as a new bride; it may be where you nursed your babies; it may even be where you gave birth. It is not unusual to feel profound sadness at having to leave all that behind, even when the house or flat now has less happy associations.

Although it's difficult to do so, try to concentrate on the future, and remember that if you've created one lovely home you will be able to create another, even if it takes a little longer and is on a more modest level.

Your partner's reaction

Most abusive men are outraged when their partners finally leave. His primary need is to maintain power and control over you, and you have challenged this by leaving him, so he is likely to be absolutely furious. Anger and outrage are often followed by disbelief – he may be so certain that he still has control over everything you do that he will expect you to 'do as you're told' and go back after a couple of days.

Charlotte
Leaving my marriage was an incredibly difficult decision and an absolute last resort. I'd tried to tell him how miserable he was

making me but he said it was my fault for not being more 'cheerful', so I used to walk around trying to smile when I felt as though I was dying inside. When I look back on it now, I can see that it was ludicrous, but I did everything I could to try and make things better, even suggesting we go to counselling. He agreed, but then got angry with the counsellor because she didn't take his side! After the counselling sessions, he'd be even worse, swearing at me because of whatever I'd said to the counsellor, telling me I was a complete idiot, a selfish bitch and a liar.

After one of these sessions, we had such an awful row that he stormed out of the house and slammed the door so hard that the glass broke. That's when I left. I rang my dad and he came and picked us up straight away. I packed whatever I could, but it didn't worry me that I had to leave loads of stuff behind – I was so unhappy by that time that I wouldn't have cared if I'd left it all behind. I left him a note saying I wasn't coming back, that I'd file for divorce in the next few days, and asking him to contact me regarding arrangements to see the children. He phoned my parents' house about a dozen times that night, demanding I come back. In the end we just took the phone off the hook. The next day he turned up at the door, and when I answered it he stood on the doorstep with his back to me, and said, 'OK, you've made your point. You can come home now.'

He couldn't believe I had actually left him. For about a week after that, he bombarded me with abusive phone calls, sometimes in the middle of the night. Then came the tears and apologies, and very briefly I felt sorry for him and thought, 'Well, maybe he really means it.' But the apologies were soon followed by accusations and blame – he'd only behaved badly because I made him angry, therefore it was my fault.

Coping with your partner's reaction can be difficult, but you can comfort yourself with the knowledge that, although the abuse may continue (see pp. 61–2), you are now in a better position to fight it. Also, there are now limits on what he can do – he no longer has access to you 24 hours a day, for a start, so instead of gradually losing your confidence and self-esteem, you can now start to rebuild it, which will make you stronger and better able to cope.

Continued abuse

Enraged by your defiance in leaving him, your partner may now mount what can seem like a planned campaign of abuse. Like Charlotte's husband, he may bombard you with aggressive phone calls or simply be verbally abusive every time you see him. Some men make silent phone calls, knowing this is likely to scare and intimidate you.

My own husband made several abusive and sometimes threatening phone calls, bombarded me with abusive notes, sometimes at the rate of four a day, and took to following me and even sitting in his car opposite the house. This was obviously very frightening and intimidating, but even though this was before 1997, when the Protection from Harassment Act (known as the 'stalking law') came into force, the police responded to my call quite quickly, gave him a ticking off and put him in a cell overnight. This kept him at bay for a while. Even more importantly, the policewoman who came to see me told me that it was very common for men to do this after their wives leave, and she reassured me that the police would always take it seriously. It was a great comfort to me to know that I was not the only one going through this, and I hope that it will be a comfort to you, too.

With the 'stalking law' in force, you are protected, in theory, from this type of behaviour. Section 2 of the Act makes it an offence to harass someone, so if his behaviour is distressing and intimidating – if, for example, he is calling you at all hours of the day and night, or sending you dozens of text messages – you should inform the police Community Safety Unit. They can issue him with a caution, and if he continues to harass you after that, he can be arrested and could face up to five years in prison.

Section 4 of the Act deals with the offence of 'causing fear of violence'. This can be more difficult to apply, because the criterion is that individual incidents must cause a fear of violence; as with emotional abuse, it is not so much 'individual incidents' that cause fear, but the behaviour when taken as a whole.

If you feel that he's stalking you, keep a detailed record of his pattern of behaviour for future reference, including, for example, the times, duration and content of telephone calls. Keep any letters or notes and photograph any damage to your property, and keep a diary recording anything that may be relevant, such as abusive language or comments, threats to hurt you or your family and so on. Keep any abusive messages left on your answering machine, and print out any abusive emails. Do not respond or enter into any conversations with him. If he's following you, make a note of the time, date and place, and his vehicle registration number. If you can do so safely, photograph him following you or hanging around outside your home, place of work, etc. A video record would be even more useful. Always take threats seriously and report them to the police – even if he has not been physically violent in the past, he may become so now, so be aware of this possibility if you have any contact with him.

Although it is likely that the abuse will get worse, and possible that your ex may become violent, in the majority of cases things will settle down, the situation will gradually improve and you will soon be able to move on and begin to enjoy your life once more. There is no point in denying that you're in for a difficult time after you leave, but with the love and support of those around you, you will become stronger and more confident as you regain control of your life. When the going gets tough, try to remember that you're not alone – ending an abusive relationship is traumatic, but you can get through it. See Chapter 7 for the inspiring stories of women who've come out the other side.

Legislation on psychological and emotional abuse

As we've seen, psychological and emotional abuse can be subtle and sometimes hard to explain, and many women are reluctant to call the police for what they may feel is a private and domestic matter. However, the law has now caught up with this concern. In March 2015, legislation was passed to tackle domestic abuse that stops short of physical assault, and to protect victims from extreme psychological and emotional abuse. The Serious Crime Bill covers the offence of 'controlling or coercive behaviour in an intimate or family relationship', and carries a maximum penalty in England and Wales of five years in prison and a fine.

Coercive and controlling behaviour was defined as the abuser preventing his or her victim from having friendships or hobbies, refusing access to money and determining many aspects of everyday life, such as when he or she is allowed to eat, sleep and go to the toilet.

The law followed a government consultation on whether the law on domestic abuse needed to be strengthened. In the consultation, 85 per cent of participants felt that the law did not provide enough protection to victims. Existing laws covered acts of violence, stalking and harassment, but didn't refer in their wording to personal relationships or the precise definition of domestic abuse.

The new law followed a campaign by Women's Aid, in partnership with the Sara Charlton Foundation and Paladin, for a law that criminalizes coercive control, psychological abuse and a pattern of domestic violence.

Research by Women's Aid found that:

- 80.4 per cent of women in refuges and 85.6 per cent of women using non-refuge services had experienced emotional abuse;
- 57.4 per cent of women in refuges and 49.7 per cent of women using non-refuge services had experienced financial abuse.

These figures are from 'Women's experiences of abuse' (April 2014), a Women's Aid survey of 522 service users of refuge services and 755 service users of non-refuge services.

A survey of survivors of domestic violence revealed:

- 88 per cent said the criminal justice system didn't take psychological harm into account and 94 per cent felt that mental cruelty can sometimes be worse than physical violence;
- 57 per cent who reported to the police mentioned more than three instances of domestic violence, but 81 per cent said that the criminal justice system did not take any pattern of abuse into account;
- 98 per cent of victims felt that reform of the law and practice concerning domestic violence is needed;
- 100 per cent felt that the police, Crime Prosecution Service, judges and magistrates should have to complete mandatory training into the dynamics and impact of domestic violence.

There were fears from some domestic violence charities such as Refuge that another law would not really help women, due to practical problems implementing it – they argued that it was difficult enough to enforce existing laws, even in cases of physical violence. A report in 2014 criticized police forces in England and Wales for failing to deal with domestic abuse adequately, and found that only eight out of 43 forces were dealing well with the issue. Organizations such as Refuge were therefore concerned that it would be hard to find evidence of, for example, controlling behaviour, which can be passed off as care or concern, and to convince judges and juries of the more subtle aspects of such behaviour. However, there are a number of ways to provide documentary evidence of controlling and coercive behaviour, such as threatening emails and text messages, and bank statements that show that the perpetrator has sought to control a victim financially. As I said in the last section, my own husband bombarded me with abusive notes – had this law been in force then, they could have provided evidence against him. Do keep careful records of texts, emails, letters, notes, and financial and other documents.

Staying safe after the split

If you feel frightened or worried by your ex-partner's continuing abusive behaviour, it may be a good idea to tell friends, family, work colleagues and the children's schools what the situation is, so that they don't inadvertently give out information to your ex.

If you have left the marital home, but remain in the same area:

- consider using a different form of transport and changing your regular routes (although make sure they're not too quiet or isolated);
- try to alter your daily routine;
- change any appointments he knows about;
- avoid places where he might expect to find you – certain supermarkets, for example.

If you have moved to a new area and need to keep your address secret:

- ask your solicitor to make sure that your address doesn't appear on court papers;
- avoid using joint bank accounts or credit cards, as the locations where they are used will show up on the statements;
- consider changing your name – you don't need to take any legal action, simply inform everyone, including your employer, tax office, GP, banks, etc. of the new name; it doesn't have to be your maiden name or have any connection with you (I picked one out of the phone book) and it will make you more difficult to trace;
- if you need to speak to your ex on the phone, dial 141 before calling – this renders the number you are calling from untraceable;

- make sure your children, and their school, understand how important it is that your location is kept confidential.

If you stay in or return to the family home, you may want to consider:

- applying to the courts for a 'non-molestation order' (see below);
- having the locks on all the doors changed – bear in mind that he may have a spare set of keys that you don't know about;
- fitting locks to all the windows;
- installing security lights outside (front and back) that come on when someone approaches;
- explaining the situation to the neighbours and asking them to alert you or to call the police if they see him nearby at times other than those where you have agreed to him collecting the children;
- changing your telephone number and screening all calls.

Non-molestation orders

You may want to consider asking the courts to grant a non-molestation order. This is aimed at preventing him from using or threatening violence against you or your children, or harassing, intimidating or pestering you. You can find out about this from your solicitor, if you have one, or from a Community Safety Unit or a Domestic Violence Advocacy Service. In most cases, your partner will be informed of your application before the court hearing, but if you're worried that this would put you or your children at increased risk of harm before you get to court, you can ask for an order 'without notification' so that he won't be told until he is served with the injunction. You may be given a temporary order until your ex can put his side of things to the court. The court will then decide whether the order should be extended.

If your ex breaches the terms of a non-molestation order, you should inform the police immediately and they should arrest him. He can be sent to prison for up to five years.

Children and contact

In the majority of cases and unless it is considered particularly dangerous, your ex-partner will continue to have contact with his children. In many cases, this works fairly well and the children benefit from continued contact with their father.

Nikki
Sam picks Kyle up on Saturdays and keeps him overnight, bringing him back on Sunday evening. It seems to be working fairly well, although Sam never misses the opportunity to have a pop at me if he can. He's now started accusing me of being an unfit mother (because I have a job and I sometimes get a babysitter so I can go out in the evening). But apart from that, it's not been too bad and my son seems to be happy. I feel so much stronger now we've separated that I can ignore his criticism a lot more easily. It's early days yet, but so far the contact visits have been relatively trouble free. I'm just hoping it stays that way!

In other cases, however, abusive men use their contact with the children as another way to continue to control their ex-partners or even to threaten and intimidate them.

Charlotte
After I left, I agreed to whatever he suggested as regards the children. But he would change arrangements at the last minute, frequently arrive up to two hours late to collect them and return them up to an hour late. Sometimes he'd just not turn up, without letting us know. The kids would spend all morning looking out of the window and then I'd have to comfort them when they finally gave up hope. It used to break my heart.

Charlotte's husband was still controlling her even after she left him. By not sticking to arrangements and being constantly late in collecting and returning the children, he was making sure that Charlotte could not relax and get on with her life.

My own husband behaved in much the same way. He once even took my children away overnight without my permission and refused to tell me where they were. He also questioned the children about my movements, told them I had wrecked his life and taken all his money and even told them he would have to go to prison because of me – it was my fault, he said, that he could no longer pay his bills. In fact, all that had happened was that, in order to stop him from using our huge overdraft as spending money, I'd asked our bank to request both signatures on cheques/withdrawals from our joint account. I would have happily authorized the paying of bills, but he never requested my signature.

If your ex behaves badly over contact, keep records of exactly what happens and keep your solicitor informed – he or she might even be able to have an informal word with your ex's solicitors with a view to getting them to make their client see that behaving badly with regard to contact visits will not go down well in court.

Unless you are genuinely concerned that your children are at risk, resist the temptation to deny your ex contact with them – this is punishing the children for his behaviour and is unlikely to solve any problems. Similarly, you should try not to burden the kids with your grievances about their dad's behaviour. Having said that, be careful not to go too far in the other direction – if you play down his bad behaviour too much, they'll wonder why you left him! The best rule to follow is honesty without too much detail. If at all possible, avoid saying, 'Don't tell Daddy' to your children. Of course, if your ex has been or is likely to be violent, you may need to ask them to keep various addresses and telephone numbers to themselves.

If you can avoid the need for them to keep certain things secret, it will be easier for you to encourage them to be honest with you about things their father has said. It is not necessary for them to relay back every insulting remark their father makes about you, but there are circumstances under which it would be better if they were able to tell you certain things: for example, if he has threatened them with punishment for not finding out something for him, or for taking your 'side' against him.

He may well use the children as a tool with which to abuse you further by means of emotional blackmail: 'Daddy says he'll kill himself if you don't come back,' or 'Daddy says he's going to take us to another country so you can't find us.' This is obviously distressing for your children and can be harmful over time.

Keeping a record of what happens may be useful should you want the courts to back your refusal of contact or your insistence that contact be supervised. Usually, courts are reluctant to support a mother who refuses contact between her children and their father. However, the judge should consider the welfare of the children first, rather than thinking about parental 'rights'. After a close look at the evidence, which may include a report by the Court Welfare Officer, the court may consider that the negative effects of distress and trauma caused by contact visits outweigh the potential benefits. Alternatively, the court may recommend supervised contact, possibly at a contact centre.

Contact centres

Child contact centres are neutral places where separated parents can spend time with their children in a child-centred environment with plenty of toys and games available. Most offer a 'handover' service so that the mother and father do not even have to see each other. Some centres, though not all, offer supervision if the children are considered to be at risk of physical or emotional harm. Most centres are affiliated to the National Association of Child Contact Centres (see Useful addresses, p. 105).

Seeing a solicitor

There are a number of matters with which you may need professional legal advice, particularly if you need protection from your partner, if you want a divorce and if there are disputes over housing, money and children.

Arrange to see a solicitor as soon as possible, preferably one experienced in matrimonial and family law. Local women's organizations or the police may be able to give you the name of a local solicitor who is experienced and sympathetic. Your local library or Citizens Advice Bureau (CAB) should have the Law Society's *Solicitors' Regional Directory*, which lists solicitors specializing in matrimonial work. You may want to take someone with you for moral support and to help you to remember what has been said – it will be difficult to take it all in, especially if you're still in a distressed state. The first appointment will probably take quite a long time as the solicitor will need to get a very clear picture of the situation in order to advise you about what your options are.

If you are unable to pay for legal services, you may be entitled to legal aid (funding through the Community Legal Service). Even if you do not qualify for legal aid, there are a number of organizations, including Citizens Advice Bureaux and Law Centres, that offer free legal advice or can advise you on getting help with legal costs. CLS Direct (see Useful addresses, p. 107) produce free leaflets on a range of legal matters.

Divorce

Once you are sure that your marriage is over, you will almost certainly want to divorce your husband, and as long as you have been married for at least one year you can start divorce proceedings on the grounds that your marriage has irretrievably broken down. There are five ways to prove 'irretrievable breakdown':

1 Your husband has committed adultery, and as a result you would find it intolerable to continue living with him (the adultery needs to have occurred within the six months before you left him).
2 Your husband's behaviour is such that you cannot reasonably be expected to go on living with him.
3 He agrees to the divorce and you and he have lived apart for at least two years.
4 You have lived apart for five years.
5 He has deserted you for two years or more.

For most women reading this, the second option will be the most appropriate (although the first may also apply). This is where your record of the abuse, if you've kept one, will come in useful. If you were unable to keep a record while you were still living with him, try to remember as much as you can now, and write it all down. If anyone else can provide evidence – your doctor, perhaps, or the police if they've been involved – this will also be useful. Friends or family members may also be able to provide evidence if they've witnessed his unreasonable behaviour, or even if they've seen your distress as a result of it. Your solicitor will use what you tell him or her to draw up a 'petition', which will provide the details of the marriage for the court, including a request that the marriage be legally dissolved and requests for financial arrangements to be made. A copy will be sent to your husband so that he has the opportunity to respond (in 'divorce-speak', the party seeking the divorce is known as 'the Petitioner' and the other party is known as 'the Respondent').

It must be said at this point that, as already mentioned, abusive men do not like to relinquish their control, and they are often as obstructive as possible when it comes to divorce. This means the process can take longer and cost considerably more than it needs to. Your husband may delay things by refusing to answer solicitors' letters; he may be deliberately obstructive when it comes to financial matters and arrangements for the children, or he may even contest the divorce. If this happens, there will need to be a court hearing where you will have to give evidence and provide witnesses to prove that the marriage has broken down irretrievably, and the onus will be on your husband to prove that it has not. These hearings are relatively rare, but they do happen.

If you find yourself in this situation you are bound to be nervous, but try not to worry. Your solicitor and/or barrister will guide you through the process and help you to give the judge a good overall picture of your husband's abusive behaviour. It is therefore very important that you provide your solicitor with as much detail as possible about what has been happening and about the effect it has had on you and on your children. This is what will show the court that your husband's behaviour is such that you cannot reasonably be expected to live with him. Remember that you are not to blame for your husband's behaviour, no matter what he has told you. When you are called to give evidence, tell the truth, answer the questions as fully and with as many examples as you can, and bear in mind that a judge hearing a case like this will have seen the situation before, and will recognize the pattern of behaviour.

Claiming benefits

You may be worried about how you'll cope financially once you've left your partner, especially if you have young children and are not able to go out to work. Your ex will be expected to make maintenance payments for the children, but abusive men often use this as another form of control – he may say that he is quite prepared to support you if you go back to him, but not if you refuse. In practice, even with a court order, it is extremely difficult to get a reluctant father to pay up and the whole issue of money becomes another battleground. There are a number of benefits you may be entitled to, such as Jobseeker's Allowance or Income Support, Housing Benefit, Council Tax Benefit, or if you work part time you may be entitled to Working Tax Credit.

If you've left home with no money, few belongings and no income, you may be able to get a Crisis Loan from the Social Fund. This is intended to cover expenses in an emergency – you do not have to be receiving any benefits to qualify for a Crisis Loan. If you are already receiving certain benefits, you may be able to claim a Budgeting Loan or a Community Care Grant. Crisis Loans and Budgeting Loans are repayable, but the loans are interest-free, so you only pay back what you borrowed. A Community Care Grant does not have to be repaid.

7

Moving on

Even when couples separate amicably and agree on financial matters and arrangements for the children, the end of the relationship can be traumatic; if the separation is acrimonious, it can be even more so. But when the relationship has been abusive, there is more to recover from. An abusive relationship, whether the abuse was physical or not, is injurious to a woman's mental and physical health, to her emotional well-being and to her sense of self. Recovering is a long and difficult process.

As mentioned in the previous chapter, you are quite likely to feel a mixture of positive and negative emotions after leaving, from relief and happiness to fear and grief. It will take a while before life gets back to normal, but it will happen, as the true stories in the second part of this chapter show. In the meantime, there are a number of ways in which you can take steps to speed up your recovery.

Looking after yourself

What you have been through will have undoubtedly taken its toll on your health, so now is the time to concentrate on taking care of yourself. Have a look at Chapter 4 for some basic, easy-to-apply advice on diet, exercise and sleep, and allow yourself a period of time to simply replenish your energy stores. You will probably have a lot of things to organize and a lot of things to worry about, but try not to rush into sorting everything out at once – you will simply exhaust yourself even more. There are some things, of course, that can't wait, but for the first week or two allow yourself to rest and sleep as much as you want to (job and children permitting). Other things that might help you to feel better are:

- relaxation exercises, such as deep breathing, meditation, visualization, etc.;
- joining a class that will help you feel more relaxed and confident as well as helping you to learn a new skill: for example, yoga, tai chi, self-defence;
- making a little time for yourself every day, even if it's just half an hour during your lunch break or while your child has a nap; during that time, try not to think about your problems and concentrate on doing something purely for pleasure: read a magazine, wallow in a scented bath, feed the ducks in the park – anything you fancy;
- taking up a creative hobby such as painting or drawing, playing an instrument or writing stories or poetry. Think about joining an adult education class – many people find art and creative writing in particular quite therapeutic in helping them recover from difficult experiences. Those who say, 'I can't write' or 'I can't paint' are often amazed at what they produce, and are surprised by the wonderful feeling of having created something original and even beautiful.

Building confidence

After living with an abusive partner, your self-confidence may be virtually non-existent. When someone you once loved and trusted frequently puts you down, criticizes you, controls your every move and abuses you verbally or physically, you start to think you are not a good person, and that you in some way deserve this treatment. If your partner made all the decisions and controlled the household finances – probably after telling you that you were too stupid to do so – you may find yourself unable to make decisions now, and you may have difficulty managing your money. This is not because you can't do these things, but because he has made you doubt your own abilities. It is scary to suddenly be responsible for areas of life that you weren't even allowed to think about before, but as you get used to living away from him you will gradually learn to trust your own judgement once more.

If you're faced with a big financial or legal decision or problem and you find yourself really struggling, it may be worth contacting an organization such as the Citizens Advice Bureau.

Often, talking about a problem or anxiety can help resolve it, so sympathetic friends or relatives may help here. Don't ask them what you should do, though, just explain that you'd simply like to talk it over. What may be even more useful is talking to someone who understands exactly what you've been through. Contact your local Women's Aid, women's outreach service or lone parent organization to see if there is a support group in your area. If not, you may want to consider setting one up.

After the way your partner treated you, you may worry that you don't have the confidence to stand up for yourself and will end up being taken advantage of in other relationships and in your dealings with various people and agencies. If this is the case, think about attending an assertiveness training class. Look in your local library or contact your local adult education institute for details – there are usually women-only classes on offer. You may also find yourself becoming increasingly angry as you think back to how he treated you; why, you ask yourself, did you let him get away with it? Logically, you know why – we've seen again and again how abusive men are able to manipulate and crush even women who have previously been strong and confident. But even though you know this, the feeling of 'unfinished business' with your ex can be very troubling. Having it out with him is not really an option – you know he won't listen – but there is a possible compromise. Some readers may regard this suggestion as a bit 'airy-fairy' or 'new-agey', but it really is worth a try: take a piece of paper and a pen, and write your ex a letter. Note: you are *not* going to send this letter, and you are not going to show it to anyone else! In fact, not only are you not going to send it or show it to anyone, but you are not even going to re-read it yourself. Just write it, say exactly what you want to, tell him how angry you are with him, call him names if you feel like it. It can be serious or it can turn into a hilarious exercise in fantasy revenge (the only healthy type of revenge!). As soon as you've finished, take the letter to a safe place outside and burn it. As the ashes float away on the breeze, so does a lot of your anger and frustration – that's the theory, anyway!

Self-confidence is closely linked with self-esteem; if you can learn to value yourself more, you'll find that your confidence increases as well. You can help the process along by getting into the right mindset. Try these tips:

- Give yourself credit for your achievements. Start with the fact that you've put an end to your abusive relationship. This is a huge and courageous step – there's not much you'll do in life that'll be harder!
- Think positive, even when it's difficult. Try to find something every day that makes you feel happy, or at least makes you smile: it could be a small kindness by someone you barely know, a beautiful sunset, a cherry tree in blossom, or watching your sleeping child. Write one thing down every day, and at the end of a week you will have seven reasons to smile!
- When you're feeling a bit low (but not too awful) trick yourself into feeling better; when someone says, 'How are things?' try saying something upbeat such as, 'Really good' or 'On the up' or even just 'Fine, thanks.' People will respond to your apparently positive mood, and before you know it, you'll genuinely feel better. (This does not, of course, mean you should deny you have problems, simply that it can be good to affirm that you are coping.)

- Think about your family, friends or work colleagues you get along well with. Now write down three things they might say they like about you – it might be something like your sense of humour, your willingness to help other people, your patience with your children or the fact that you're a good listener.
- Write down three things you're good at – can you draw, paint, dance or sing? Are you a great cook? Do you have a flair for home decorating or interior design? Maybe you can take cuttings from any plant and make them grow. Perhaps you're really good at organizing things, or maybe you're a fantastic driver. It doesn't matter how 'everyday' the skills are, just that you recognize them as things you're good at.
- Try to be nice to other people, even when you feel you hate the world. If you can do a small kindness to someone or pay them a compliment, they'll view you as a nice person, which will improve the way you view yourself.

Your new life

After years of worrying about upsetting or angering your partner by having a social life, going to work, furthering your education or in fact making any choices he didn't approve of, you now have only yourself and the children to think about. It can be scary to suddenly be making your own choices and decisions, but it is also an exciting time, and the difficult parts will become easier over the coming weeks and months. You don't need to rush into anything, so allow yourself to recover a little and start to think about your future when you feel up to it. If you have access to the internet (your local library will usually have internet access if you don't have a computer at home) have a look at <www.singleparents.org.uk> or <www.oneparentfamilies.org.uk> for lots of advice on lone parenting and related issues, such as work, childcare, claiming benefits and returning to education.

If you have young children, it may not be viable for

you to take full-time employment, although it might be worth taking a part-time job and claiming a benefit such as Working Tax Credit. Contact the Citizens Advice Bureau or National Benefits Helpline for more information on benefits (see Useful addresses, p. 107). If you have been working but have had to leave your job because you've moved to a new area or gone into a refuge, you may want to look for a similar job, or you may want to think about doing something completely different. Perhaps now is the time to re-train for the career you've always dreamed of, or maybe you could use this opportunity to go back to 'school' to gain GCSEs, A levels or a degree. Whether you study for academic or vocational qualifications, furthering your education can be very empowering and will extend your range of choices, enhance your social life and improve your confidence and sense of self-worth. Whatever you decide to do, it's *your* choice.

Helping the children

Your children will be affected by what has happened, in terms of both the abusive relationship and the trauma of leaving it. They will probably have had to leave many toys or posses-sions behind, and if you've moved to a new area there will be the additional wrench of leaving their school and friends. Even if he was abusive to them as well as you, they will almost certainly miss their dad, and may turn on you for taking them away from him. Hopefully, they will be able to maintain a relationship with him if it is considered safe for them to do so (see pp. 65–7).

Coping with their distress can be difficult when you're still traumatized yourself, but it can also be a useful focus and even a distraction. Try to establish a daily routine that's as 'normal' as possible under the circumstances. They will feel unsettled and insecure, so it's important to show them that you are there for them, providing a stable, loving home even if it's not the place they know as 'home'. Encourage them to share their concerns and answer their questions as honestly as you can.

If they're reluctant to talk, it may be useful to set aside a little 'special time' every day. At a specific time, perhaps in the evening when they're winding down, allocate five or ten minutes' 'special time' for each child. With just you and your child present, and preferably no distractions around such as television or other children, start by saying a little about how you're feeling. Identify one emotion, starting with, 'I'm feeling ...' (sad, happy, excited, tired, etc.) and follow this with a brief explanation of why you might feel like this. It's important not to go into too much detail, especially when talking about negative emotions, because you don't want to burden your child. You could, for example, relate feeling sad to a storyline in a book or TV programme. You could also use real-life examples, as long as they're not too worrying for the child – perhaps something to do with work or friendships. After you've done this, tell your child it's his or her turn. It's important for you to listen carefully, but to still appear relaxed while your child is speaking. They may prefer to hide or cover their face, or they may prefer it if you look the other way. Some children will be happier talking to you while they're engaged in some other activity such as drawing or colouring. This may be the only way to get them to talk, but once they're comfortable with the routine, try to encourage a more focused, separate time.

'Special time' allows the child to identify emotions effectively – some children can identify sadness more easily than anger, for example. It will show them that it's OK to feel sad/angry/frightened or whatever, and it will give you the opportunity to reassure them. It can be a good idea to pick up on the child's emotion and link it with a memory of feeling the same: for example, 'I remember when I felt sad at school, too.' It is good for children to understand that not all emotions are negative, so it could be helpful to suggest one 'good' emotion and one 'bad'.

If your child doesn't want to say any more after the 'I'm feeling ...', don't worry. And don't push the issue, just give the same opportunity the following evening. Similarly, your child may start talking about something apparently unrelated. Again, don't force the issue, but you could try saying something like, 'I'd really like to hear all about that in a minute, but can we do special time first?' Once a routine is established, you may find your child is impatient for you to finish your turn so that he or she can get started!

'Special time' can help to 'unclog' a build-up of anger, frustration or other negative emotion, and can be particularly useful for boys who find talking about feelings and emotions difficult.

I wish I had been introduced to the idea of 'special time' when my own children were going through this. I made a huge mistake in thinking that my son, then seven, was relatively unaffected by what had happened, because while his older sister screamed, cried and said she hated me, he sat quietly, did as he was told and never cried. Both children were damaged by the experience, but my daughter, now in her thirties, agrees that being able to express her feelings at the time helped her to cope, whereas it took her younger brother a little longer.

Make use (or encourage your children to do so) of other sources of support, such as grandparents or other relatives, friends, teachers, youth workers, etc. Not only will this provide extra support for your children, but it will relieve you of some of the burden. You may also consider encouraging them to have a look at the website run by Women's Aid for children and young people who have witnessed physical or non-physical abuse or are still living in a situation where this is taking place: <www.thehideout.org.uk>. Another useful organization is Young Minds, which is an information service for parents worried about a young person's mental health. They produce a range of leaflets, including one on the effects of divorce and separation on young people.

One other problem you might experience with your children is that they seem to have lost respect for you and for your authority as a parent. This stems directly from what they have observed in terms of the way your ex treated you in front of them. Children learn by example, and even though they love you and will have been upset by the way their dad treated you, they may still have picked up his subtle way of undermining you and putting you down. In my own case, this was something my family noticed soon after I left my ex. They helped by encouraging me to make lots of small decisions regarding the children in order to re-establish my authority and status as a parent: for example, 'Grandma, can I have a biscuit?'

'Ask Mummy, she's in charge.'

I was so weakened and vulnerable for those first few weeks that I would probably not have noticed this myself, and it would have become an even bigger problem had it not been addressed so quickly. It's as well to be aware of this possibility so that you can enlist the help of family and friends in dealing with it if necessary.

It will be difficult for your children to settle in their new situation, as it will be for you. But with your love and support, a stable, non-abusive environment and continued reassurance that things will get better, your children will gradually recover and will become happier and more confident as time goes on.

More stories

Throughout this book, you have read excerpts from interviews with women who have experienced abusive relationships with men they once loved. All the women who responded to my request for interviewees had already left their relationships, some recently, some many years ago. Many were hesitant and apologetic when they contacted me: 'It wasn't really *abuse*,' they said, and then went on to describe the years of abject misery and fear they suffered at the hands of controlling, bullying and even violent partners. It seems that even away from our abusive partners, we have trouble recognizing what happened to us as abuse. It is only, perhaps, when we hear what happened to other women, when we recognize the anguish and self-doubt, and when we see that the familiar types of behaviour form a pattern, that we begin to accept the reality of the situation. It is for this reason that the second part of this chapter is made up of the accounts of women who have experienced emotional, psychological, verbal and, indeed, physical abuse.

In reading these stories, you may recognize your own situation, one that you may still be enduring. Whether you are still suffering abuse or whether the relationship is now behind you, I hope that you will take comfort from the knowledge that there are many women out there who know exactly how you feel and what you've been through. I hope, also, that you will be encouraged by their tales of survival and recovery, of achievement in education or career, of new or renewed friendships and, in some cases, of new love and well-deserved, long-awaited happiness.

Sara's story

As soon as I moved in with Sean, I realized how controlling he was. He'd sort through all my clothes and tell me what I could and couldn't wear when I was with him. He was always angry about something – I couldn't seem to do anything right, and he'd hold my wrists or arms while he was shouting at me so that I couldn't get away. He wouldn't allow my best friend in the house, because he didn't like her 'attitude' – she'd seen him for what he was. I actually lost touch with her because of him, although happily we're back in touch now.

After about six months, I couldn't stand it any more and I moved out, but he came to where I was staying and begged me to come back.

He was crying; he said he loved me and he was sorry. I felt sorry for him, and I went back. We found another place to live, but things soon became bad again. At one point, when I said I wanted to live on my own, he went mad; he knelt on my neck and put his hands over my nose and mouth; I really thought he was going to kill me. It shook him up too, though, and soon after, he told me that the doctor had said he was depressed, so it wasn't his fault. We lived separately for a while, which helped, but then we moved in together again.

Things got worse. He bullied me into writing his dissertation as well as my own – I missed a first-class degree by two marks as a result. He told me I was 'selfish' so often that I began to think maybe I was and maybe everything was my fault. He borrowed money from me which he never paid back, he criticized me constantly, moving furniture out to see if I'd vacuumed behind it, complaining about the cat being 'too hairy' – he wanted me to vacuum her! I told him you couldn't vacuum a cat and not to be ridiculous, but the next time I got the vacuum cleaner out, the cat ran and hid under the bed, so I'm fairly sure that's what he did. He even criticized the food I cooked. Once, I'd planned to cook fish with mashed potatoes, leeks and cheese sauce. I was due to go to a meeting to do with work and was running late, so I said we'd better have something else. He insisted I had time to cook the meal and made it very clear that he'd be angry if I didn't. So I spent ages preparing this meal and making myself late, and when I put it in front of him he yelled at me because my 'presentation' wasn't good enough.

He became increasingly abusive until, eventually, I had a revelation: I realized that he couldn't possibly love me, that other people's lives weren't like this, and that out of the two years we'd been together, I'd only been happy for about a week and a half. I told him it was over, and that I wanted him to move out. I did all I could to stay away from him. I tried to be out by the time he got home and I'd come back at about 3 a.m. and sleep on the sofa. If he was there when I had to eat, I'd eat my meals in the bathroom.

When I met Marc, who is now my husband, I quickly realized he was my soul-mate. I saw a lot of Marc, but Sean was still living in the flat so I couldn't take him back there. We decided to spend a weekend away together but I didn't dare tell Sean, even though we were no longer an item. I was worried about what he might do – he'd been making horrible remarks about the cat and eyeing her in a nasty way, and I was worried he'd hurt her (he once told me he'd tried to strangle a cat) so I told him I was staying with a girlfriend.

While we were away, I turned my mobile on to find ten messages, one from the friend I'd said I was staying with, and nine from Sean. He'd pestered my friend with calls and had threatened her, and the messages he'd left for me were all full of abuse and threats to kill himself.

That's when I knew I had to get out. I went to my parents' and asked my brother if he'd go with me to pick up the cat and my stuff. He agreed, but I could tell he thought I was exaggerating. When we went in, Sean was sitting on the floor, unshaven and dishevelled, cutting my head out of every photograph in the place. My brother was finally convinced!

Shortly after that, Sean emailed Marc and threatened to kill him. The police were great. They kept him in the cells overnight, although they couldn't charge him because he immediately said sorry and that it was a stupid thing to have said. The next morning, they kept phoning me to check that I'd got my stuff out and was away from the flat before they let him go.

For a while, we had email contact (his were mostly abusive) over the £3,000 he owes me. I considered taking him to the small claims court, but in the end I decided that it was a small price to pay for getting my life back.

I feel I began to blossom as soon as I left Sean. Marc and I have been happily married for four years now, and sometimes I still can't believe how easy the relationship is: no shouting, no stress – it's wonderful! It took a while for me to get my confidence back as far as work was concerned, but I now run my own successful PR company, and I'm very happy. When I look back, I can't quite believe what I put up with.

Rebecca's story

I was only 16 when I met David, and he just swept me off my feet – he was quite a bit older than me and very wealthy and successful. For the first few years we had a great time: we travelled, went to the best restaurants and he bought me clothes and diamonds. I knew he had an unpleasant side, but I ignored it because I was blown away by the lifestyle – parties with expensive food and pink champagne, fabulous holidays and, eventually, a gorgeous house. I assumed I had to take the rough with the smooth. I didn't notice at first how controlling he was – he had great taste, so I didn't mind when he told me what clothes to wear and how I should do my hair.

My friend noticed that he was often critical and unreasonable, but when she mentioned it I suppose I didn't want to listen, so I said she was wrong. He started to become verbally abusive, especially after he'd been drinking, and would belittle me, bragging about his own achievements and telling me I was useless and incompetent. He never asked my opinion about anything, and I realized that I was at the bottom of a hierarchy that had him at the top, then our 18-month-old daughter, then his mother, then me. I wanted to do a make-up course at one point, but he wouldn't let me – he told me my job was looking after the house.

He was very particular about things – everything had to be absolutely perfect, and if I had friends over we'd be terrified in case we spilled a drink on the carpet. He was very strict about his meals – everything had to be done the 'right' way, and if it wasn't perfect he'd make sarcastic comments and then go on about how I'd ruined perfectly good food. He seemed to be even worse in front of other people, as though he got a real kick out of criticizing and insulting me.

One night, just after our second daughter was born, he got so blind drunk he could hardly stand, and then he decided he wanted to take our newborn in the car and drive to his mum's. I said 'no' and he was furious. I remember phoning his mum in such a panic that I could hardly breathe. Fortunately, she spoke to him and managed to calm him down and talk some sense into him.

He always wanted me to party with him but, of course, once I had the children it was less practical, and I was often tired. On our wedding anniversary, we were in Rome in a fantastic restaurant, and I said I didn't want to drink any more wine because I knew I'd have to be up for about 6 a.m. with the kids, who were both under three. He looked at me icily and said, 'Have a drink, bitch.' I said, 'Look, I really don't want to, and anyway, who do you think you're talking to?' He replied, 'Only a f***ing car dealer's daughter.'

I realized after a while that I was just living for the time I could be away from him. I'd started to dread him coming home, and I hated the fact that the children would see and hear him abusing me.

Eventually, it became physical. On one occasion, he started on me when I was just about to go out. We were in the hall and I had the two children strapped into their buggy. As he was trying to strangle me, I could see my daughter, then just under three, beginning to panic; she and the baby were both crying but David ignored them. My daughter still remembers this – she's 12 now. On another occasion, he pulled me off the bed by my hair, and on another, I climbed out of a ground-floor window and ran barefoot across sharp stones and rubble (we were having the drive re-laid) and scaled a six-foot wall to get away from him. Again he got hold of me by the hair and dragged me back.

I called the police on several occasions, and eventually they advised me to leave.

After I left, it took ages to get a settlement, but when I did, I set up my own property business – something I'd wanted to do for years, but which David always ridiculed. It's now going really well, and I'm proud of my achievements. It's eight years since I left him, and I think it took me a good five years to get over it, including two years of counselling, which I found very helpful. I adored David and I trusted him, but when I look back at how he treated me, I can't believe I stayed with him as long as I did.

Melanie's story

Bob did become violent in the end, but for years it was what I'd call mental torture. I still find it difficult to talk about, and it has affected me so badly that I'm on a lot of medication for depression. He died last year – probably suicide, we don't know for sure – but up until then I was trapped. I knew I had to get out of the relationship but I'd no idea how.

I had a very unhappy childhood, and Bob was the first person who ever loved me, so I put a lot of trust in him even though he was married. Even when we were first together, he wouldn't let me go out on my own, and he'd only let me wear a skirt when I was with him – he said he didn't want other men looking at me. I thought he must really adore me and that he was terrified of losing me. But then he told me he wanted me to sleep with his friend. I said no at first, but he kept on and on at me, saying that if I loved him, I'd do it. I told him I didn't want to, but he said I obviously didn't love him and so we might as well split up. I was terrified he'd leave me, and so I did what he said. I know it sounds unbelievable, but I honestly thought he must be right; I thought that if you really loved someone, you'd do anything for them. It never occurred to me that it was supposed to work both ways round.

After I fell pregnant, I became even more terrified that he'd leave me, so I tried harder to please him. This was very difficult, because most of the time it seemed as though I couldn't do anything right. No matter what I did, it seemed I was doing it the wrong way. One day, he wanted coffee while I was changing the baby's nappy; I said I'd do it when I'd finished, but he yelled at me, 'Do it now!' Then he complained that I hadn't made it right and hadn't made it quickly enough.

After I had the children I wasn't working, so I relied on him totally for money, but he only ever gave me the bare minimum. Sometimes he'd leave me with no money for days, and I'd end up borrowing £5 here and there from a neighbour or friend. I could never take the kids out, partly because I didn't have enough money, but also because he didn't like me going out at all. Even if we had a day in the park, I'd have to tell the kids not to tell Daddy. My life revolved around him completely – every single thing I did, I had to think, 'Will this be OK with Bob?'

I was so dependent on him and so scared that he'd leave me and the kids to fend for ourselves – which is what he kept threatening – that I put up with anything, even when some part of me was saying, 'This isn't right. This isn't *normal*.' But I'd never been out with anybody before Bob, and I just wasn't sure. He'd criticized me so much that I felt I *must* be to blame. I certainly didn't trust my own judgement.

Over the years, things got worse. He was seeing other women and even brought them into our home, and he made me do things that I can't even talk about, simply by making me believe that I was abnormal for not wanting to. He started to slap me when I didn't do what he wanted or didn't do it quickly enough, then the slaps turned into beatings, and sometimes he raped me as well. In between, though, he'd tell me that he loved me and the kids, and part of me believed him – because I wanted to believe him, I suppose. I kept hoping it would get better, but it didn't. I suffered some pretty severe beatings, but I think the mental and psychological torture was as bad, if not worse.

His death was a terrible shock, and I think the only thing that kept me going was having to get the kids to school each day. Bob had controlled my life to such an extent that I didn't know how to exist on my own, and it was terrifying to have to make decisions, even minor ones. I'm only just beginning to get used to the idea that I can do things without asking his permission – I know that seems crazy for a woman in her thirties, but that's how my life was.

I've moved house now, and the kids seem happier. I'm getting a lot of support from a local lone parent organization called Lone Parents (see Useful addresses, p. 105) and I'm having some counselling, although I find it very difficult because I'm so used to hiding my feelings. I don't know how long it will take me to recover, and at the moment I have good days and bad days. I'm just going to take one day at a time.

Vicky's story

Glen seemed so normal at first, but when I look back I can see that there were warning signs. I remember one occasion in particular. We'd been together for about a year, and I came home one evening to find him sitting in my flat (he had a spare key) even though we hadn't made arrangements to meet. He was furious that I hadn't been there waiting for him, even though I'd no idea he was coming. I told him that if I'd have known, I'd have changed my plans and come home, but he was still unreasonably angry. I remember thinking, 'This is odd,' but he was so nice the rest of the time that it didn't seem like a big deal.

But then things like that started happening more and more. Not long after we were married, I'd arranged a 'girls' night' with a couple of friends – nothing wild, just the three of us having a laugh watching the Eurovision Song Contest on the telly with a couple of bottles of wine and a few nibbles. I told Glen exactly where I was going and what time I'd be back. But when I came home, the living room floor was covered with CDs and chunks of plaster and bits of wood – he'd kicked the shelf off the wall in a temper because, he said, he didn't know where I was.

He'd often say I hadn't told him things when I knew I had, and soon he started claiming he'd told *me* something when I knew he hadn't. He did this so much that I started to question myself – I thought I was going mad.

One of the things that used to upset me the most, though, was when he'd phone me at work and say something like, 'Let's go for a meal/ drink/to see a film.' I'd agree, go home, get showered and ready to go out, and then he wouldn't turn up. Sometimes he'd say he'd meet me at the restaurant or pub or whatever, so I'd turn up and wait, feeling a fool. I'd phone him and he'd tell me he'd be there in a minute, but he never came, and would eventually come home after closing time having obviously been out with his mates. I told him that if he wanted to go out with his mates that was fine, but why did he keep making arrangements with me and then breaking them? He'd then become aggressive, shouting and swearing at me, saying I was totally paranoid. He'd tell lies, spend money behind my back and sometimes stay out all night (claiming he'd fallen asleep on the bus on the way home from work), but if I said anything he'd go berserk. I don't know how he did it, but he used to make me feel as though I was being irrational for being upset about behaviour that was completely unreasonable. I can see now that it was all designed to control me.

I left him once, but he managed to convince me that we could try again so I went back, although not for long. During that time a lot happened: I became pregnant, my father died and things between Glen and me became much worse. He moved out because he thought I needed 'space to grieve' for my dad, but he kept coming to the house, sometimes letting himself in while I was in bed. He was more aggressive and abusive than ever.

About three months after my father died, Glen rang me in the early hours of the morning to tell me that our marriage wasn't working because all I could think about was 'babies and dead dads'. He'd lose his temper and smash things up, especially anything to do with the baby. He became physically violent with me as well. He'd slapped me a couple of times over the years, but nothing like this. He punched me in the stomach, head-butted me and was extremely threatening even without actually hitting me – once, he held me by the hair and smashed his fist into the wall beside me so close that I felt it skim my face. Another time, I picked up a knife to move it out of his way; he grabbed it, cutting himself in the process, then he pinned me up against the sink and slowly wiped the blood all over my face.

Both my midwife and my priest told me they feared for my own and my baby's safety if I continued to have contact with Glen. His aggression definitely got worse when I became pregnant. We finally separated when I was 20 weeks pregnant. My son was born 17 days late, and I often wonder whether that was because I was so scared of Glen that I was subconsciously trying to keep the baby safe inside me.

We've been divorced for four years now, but he's still trying to control and intimidate me. He packed all his stuff ready to move out but wouldn't actually move it, so he had to keep coming back to get things. He'd drag a box into the middle of the lounge, take out what he wanted and just leave the box there, so I'd come home from work once or twice a week and find his stuff spilling out all over the floor.

I bent over backwards to arrange things so that he could have contact with our son, who's now three, but he wouldn't turn up when he was supposed to, he ignored Jamie's birthdays and didn't even send him a Christmas card. Then he'd ring up and scream at me that I was denying him the right to see his son. He'd say our marriage only ended because I'd pushed him away and because I hadn't grown up. Sometimes, when he phoned, I'd know that there was someone in the room with him, because he'd be talking calmly, and saying things like, 'Vicky, stop shouting at me,' or 'Vicky, why do you say these horrible things?' when all the time I was perfectly calm and asking him what he was talking about.

He's not seen Jamie for a year now, and has only been in touch to swear at me or send abusive texts: 'You filthy bitch, I hope you rot in hell.' As far as I'm concerned, that's it now. He's clearly not interested in his son, and Jamie doesn't even know who he is. I don't want any contact at all with him now. I've moved to a new house in a different city; I've changed my phone numbers and I have a new job. I'm also studying for a degree – something he would never have allowed me to do – and I'm slowly getting my life back together. I used to be a confident, outgoing person before I met Glen, but I'm much more wary now, especially of men. I've been asked out a few times, but I don't really feel I can trust men I don't know. I hope that will change, but in the meantime I'm happy to be single, enjoying my son and finishing my degree. Life is so much better!

Shirley's story

I met Terry on holiday. We were quite young, and everybody was drinking heavily – it was one of those boozy nights, everyone having a good time and ripe for a holiday romance. But when we got back home, we stayed together. Terry was a plumber and he worked really hard. He seemed to be kind and supportive, and everyone thought he was very charming and a 'good catch'.

But the heavy drinking continued, and after our first child was born it got worse. He was verbally abusive at first, shouting at me and swearing. I hated him using bad language but that seemed to make him do it all the more. He couldn't control his anger and would take it out on things around him – he'd smash furniture, punch doors, kick things. He seemed to be getting more and more aggressive as time went on, and there wasn't even any affection in between. Sex was awful – I had to psych myself up beforehand, and once, when I didn't feel like it, he forced himself on me.

I can see now that he just couldn't handle stress, or anything bad. When I was in labour, for example, he came into the labour ward eating a kebab. When I asked him if he would rub my back to relieve the pain, he threw the kebab at me. He admitted afterwards that the whole thing had shocked him, and that he didn't know how to cope. When the boys were small, he'd smack them if they were naughty – I didn't approve of smacking any-way – but it was as if he couldn't stop, he just kept hitting and hitting them, and I'd have to get in between them and stop it. I left him once, and he came chasing after me with flowers and promises and I believed him, but after a couple of good weeks he was back to normal again.

He became physically violent towards me on a few occasions. Once, he half-strangled me in front of our five-year-old son (he's 20 now but he still remembers it). I'd popped down to the video shop, and in the half hour that I was out, Terry had drunk a whole bottle of wine. I said something like, 'Did you have to drink that much?' and he went for me. He had his hands around my throat and slammed me up against the wall. My son says he remembers seeing my feet dangling above the ground.

I think what saved me was going back to education. I'd been a complete failure at school, and so I had a very low opinion of myself and low expectations of how I should be treated. But I remember one day, after Terry had wet the bed again because he was so drunk, I thought, 'This could be the rest of my life if I don't do something about it.' So I started an access course, followed by a degree in psychology and, eventually, a PhD. I found education very empowering, and it gave me a lot more confidence, but Terry's behaviour was taking a real toll on me. I developed a nervous facial twitch, and I started having anxiety attacks when I suspected things were going to kick off.

Things came to a head after I consulted a well-respected hypnotherapist for help with my lack of sexual desire. I was extremely vulnerable at the time and I trusted this man completely. I disclosed some very personal things, told him stuff about my childhood and other intimate details. I trusted him completely. During what was supposed to be the final session, he tricked me into having sex with him. I knew straight away that he'd taken advantage of me – I'd never have slept with him normally. Apart from anything else, he was an unattractive man in his sixties and I was a young woman. I told Terry what had happened immediately. I couldn't get this man removed from the register of approved hypnotherapists because of who he was. I did go to a newspaper, though, and after investigating, they did a full-page spread on the story, which should have made sure that his other clients saw him for what he was.

Terry was furious, understandably, but he never forgave me, even though it was made very clear that I hadn't been to blame. One night a few months after this happened, I was in the bath when Terry kicked the door open and told me I had 60 seconds to get out. The kids were all standing there. Terry was drunk, of course. He said, 'Mummy slept with another man without using a condom and now I might have AIDS.'

So I left. And it really was the best thing I ever did, apart from the fact that he continued to use the boys to hurt and manipulate me. He'd tell them things like, 'Mummy is a whore' and once, a couple of years after I left, when my son, then ten, happened to mention that I was seeing someone, Terry said, 'I'm surprised anyone would want to go near that worn-out old fanny.' That was typical of his vile, crude comments. He seemed to set out to take away my dignity and to make the boys lose respect for me as a mother.

Unfortunately, at the age of 13 my youngest son decided to go back and live with his dad, possibly because he was the most susceptible to the way his father badmouthed me. Terry still drinks, and I know he hits

Luke, who's 16 now. Since going to live with his father, Luke has been expelled from school, he's been in trouble with the police several times and he's been arrested twice. But Terry still has shared residency. Every time I tried to challenge it, I was told what a nice, charming man he seemed. My older boys, now 18 and 20, are doing well and don't want contact with their dad. I just hope Luke isn't too badly damaged in the end.

Lindsay's story

I wasn't with Paul for very long – less than a year – but during that time he changed my personality completely. Before I met him, I would have described myself as being outgoing, decisive and even headstrong. I was popular and socially confident, but Paul almost destroyed me.

He would chip away at my confidence the whole time and frequently belittle me in front of people. We worked together in a bar for a while, and if I was serving a customer, especially if it was a pretty girl, he'd come and say something like, 'Are you having trouble there?' and then he'd take over the transaction, as though I couldn't handle it on my own. He'd subtly criticize everything I did, said or wore, even down to my lipstick or perfume, saying things like, 'Are you sure you want to wear that?' If I offered an opinion on something, he'd laugh and shake his head as though it was the most ridiculous thing he'd ever heard. He borrowed money from me, which I never got back.

If I displeased him in any way – say we were out shopping, for example, and I wanted to go home because I was tired – he would fly into a terrible rage. His face would be red with fury, his fists would be clenched and he'd push his face right into mine and just scream at me. I got used to people coming up to me in the street and asking if I was all right. It was truly terrifying. At home, it seemed more of a controlled rage, and he'd use a stern voice, as though he was the parent or teacher and I was the child. He was never physically violent, but I was afraid he would eventually become so – I just couldn't see how that level of rage could be contained.

My friends and family started to comment on the change in me, on the fact that I was always on edge when I was with him, and that he would belittle me in front of them. After we'd been together for about six months I tried to end it, but he just dissolved into tears, said he loved me, he was sorry, he would never hurt me and so on. He begged me not to leave him, and I thought, 'Well, maybe I'm the one who's got it all wrong,' so we tried again. But it got worse. I couldn't do anything right. I made sure I didn't do things that I knew would upset him, so I stopped going out and seeing my friends. Eventually, I became so low that I went to the doctor and was diagnosed with depression. When I told Paul I'd been prescribed antidepressants he was livid, saying how could I put him under this pressure and didn't he have enough to cope with without my problems!

Eventually, while I was staying at my mum's, we had this massive row over the phone, and he said, 'Let's just split up then.' I said, 'OK' – I'd never have said it to his face, but being away from him I felt stronger. He was furious – he obviously expected me to beg and plead with him to stay with me. Soon after that, I bumped into a friend and told her we'd split. She was relieved – she said it was the best thing I'd ever done and that everyone who knew me had been really worried.

But even after the relationship was over, he still managed to affect my life. He spread a lot of rumours, and told people we both knew very intimate details about me. He told his parents I was mad, and when he heard I was in a new relationship he started spreading lies about my new boyfriend.

I was on antidepressants for quite a long time after the relationship ended six years ago, but I'm off them now and I'm becoming stronger all the time, although I'm not sure I'll ever be completely back to normal. A while ago, for example, I was supposed to be driving my boyfriend somewhere and we walked quite a way to where the car was parked, only to find that I'd forgotten the keys. I almost broke down – I was saying things like, 'I'm so stupid,' 'How could I have done this?' , and 'It's all my fault,' and so on. My boyfriend was horrified. He said, 'You forgot the keys, so what? I'll be a bit late – it doesn't matter, and I'm grateful that you're driving me anyway.' I could hardly believe there wasn't going to be a big argument about it, which is ridiculous because my boyfriend would never treat me like that. The thing is, I'd got so used to being shouted at and blamed for everything that I automatically gave myself a hard time for any tiny mistake.

I'm getting better, but I find my confidence is still not quite there. I think I come over as being fairly confident, especially at work, but I find I need lots of positive feedback all the time. I've become very 'results-focused' – if I can't actually see that I'm doing a good job, and if somebody isn't telling me fairly frequently, then I start to doubt myself. I'd say I'm about 90 per cent the girl I was before I met him, but I've still got a little way to go.

Jenny's story

I always knew Gary drank heavily, even before we were married, but he was what I'd always thought of as a 'happy drunk', the life and soul of the party. I knew his drinking was a problem, but I was so desperate for affection I married him anyway. Then his younger brother died, and that changed everything – he became a totally different person.

We lived near the area where I grew up, so I often bumped into people I went to school with. But if I said hello to any man, Gary would accuse me of having an affair. Even when I explained that it was someone I knew from school or a neighbour or whatever, he'd call me a whore and a slut, and say that everybody knew what I was like. He'd become very insecure since his brother died, but he seemed to take it out on me. He criticized me and put me down constantly, and the jealousy became unbearable. He was accusing me of sleeping with every man I came into contact with – men at work, men I'd been to school with, even men who simply walked past me in the street. I tried pointing out how illogical and irrational his fears were – I didn't have the *time* to have an affair, never mind the inclination; the children were always with me, so there was no way I could have seen anyone else – but he still didn't believe me; he'd convinced himself that it was true. I used to have to walk around looking at the pavement, because if I looked up and there were any men around, Gary would say I was looking at them and did I think he was stupid or something?

I soon stopped seeing all my friends because Gary didn't approve of any of them – he thought they were 'a bad influence' and he'd say stuff like, 'Why do you want to spend time with her? You know she goes with men.' Which wasn't true – I think he just wanted to cut me off so that I couldn't tell people how he was behaving.

Gary wasn't a happy drunk any more, and things were always worse when he was drunk. Then he became physically violent as well. One day, I was supposed to be at a meeting to do with work, and a colleague sent me a text to see where I was. Gary was convinced it was evidence I was having an affair. He went completely mad, pulling me around the house by the hair. Another time, I was just coming into the house when someone I'd been to primary school with walked past and we said hello; Gary was watching out of the window and he went berserk. Someone called the police, and when they arrived he actually attacked the police officer. As a result, he ended up in court and they recommended a 'domestic abuse offenders' programme', which he agreed to go on. But when the time came they wouldn't let him take part because he still hadn't dealt with his drinking, so of course things didn't get any better.

One day, in the course of the voluntary work I was doing at the time, I accompanied a client who was looking for a place in a women's refuge. As she was talking to the workers at the refuge about her abusive relationship, I just thought, 'Why am I putting up with this?' It all sounded so familiar. One morning soon after that, after he'd gone to work, I packed a bag, took the kids and went to a refuge myself.

That was a couple of years ago now, and I am gradually recovering, although the whole thing with Gary has really knocked my confidence. For a long time, I honestly believed that I must be worthless or he wouldn't have treated me like that. Even now, if someone pays me a compliment, I think, 'Liar.' I've had to give up my lovely home, and although I'm glad to have somewhere safe to live, there's no garden for the kids to play in, and it's not a very nice place. Gary is still being difficult – he comes to the house, supposedly to see the kids but he just wants to keep an eye on me. He pays no attention to the kids when he's with them, and they know he's not interested – I have to bribe my daughter to even talk to her dad on the phone.

But at least he can't intimidate me any more. I feel so much stronger now I'm away from him. I'm planning to stay single now. I love being a mother and I want to concentrate on giving my children the attention they deserve. I'm studying for a diploma at the local college and I've been 'invited to apply' for a job I'm really keen on, so even though things aren't totally back to normal, they're certainly looking up!

The final story is slightly different from the others included here. The abuse Debbie suffered was physical right from the start, although some of the mental abuse, she says, was almost as painful. I have included her story as an example of how a woman can regain control of her life even after the most horrific abuse almost destroyed it. As Debbie says, 'If I can do it, anyone can!'

Debbie's story

I grew up in a violent household, so when my boyfriend first became violent it seemed almost normal. I wasn't allowed to talk to anyone or see anyone – he kept me locked in the house. If we needed any shopping, he'd come with me to make sure I didn't talk to anyone. He would bring men and women back to the house, have sex with them and make me have sex with them. Sometimes he'd film what was happening. I was beaten, raped and stabbed, but he was so charming to everyone else that no-one believed me when I told them. I tried to tell my family, but he told them I was mad, that I'd been seeing a psychiatrist and I was on medication that made me delusional. Once, the neighbours called the police because they could hear him beating me, but by the time they arrived he'd turned all the lights out so they couldn't see in. I remember seeing them through the window while he raped me with his hand stuffed in my mouth so I couldn't scream.

I tried to kill myself, but even then he managed to convince the hospital staff that I was lying about the abuse. Eventually, something snapped, and while he was drunk one night I took his keys, unlocked the front door and ran.

I was away, but I didn't ask anyone for help, because I didn't know how to have a conversation. I'd lived in a silent world for all those years, and I just didn't know how to talk.

After sleeping rough for a while, I met my Mike. I couldn't have been more vulnerable at that point, and I thought he was going to look after me, but he started abusing me too. He was violent from the start, but I was used to that – I thought it was normal. But I'd never experienced the mental games before, and that was when I really did start to question my sanity. He'd move things around in the flat while I was out. Once, he actually took a mirror off the wall and replaced it with a smaller one. When I asked him about it, he laughed and said I must be 'losing it'. He'd tell me I'd done things I knew I hadn't, or that I hadn't done things I knew I had, and he started getting rid of items of clothing, then swear blind I'd never even owned such an item.

It was only after my second child was born that I started to get a grip on my life. It was when the health visitor came to see the baby that it started to come to a head. She could see that all was not well, and when I started telling her what had been going on she put me in touch with a support worker from a local lone parent organization, and my life started to change from there. Just by taking part in their mentoring scheme, which involved me going in regularly and talking through my situation, I started to realize that I didn't have to take this any more. I threw him out, but he kept coming round, saying he wanted to move back in. One day, he kicked the door in and attacked me in front of the kids. I tried to dial 999 on my mobile, but he tore it away from me, then took the SIM card out and swallowed it!

After that, I got an injunction out against him. It said he could stand on the other side of the road to my house, but he wasn't to walk across. So what he did was to stand there, day after day, watching and intimidating me. Once or twice, I knew he'd been in my flat because I'd come back and find footprints on the carpet when I knew they hadn't been there before.

But as I became stronger, he was less and less able to intimidate me, and when I look back I can't believe I allowed it to continue – not only the violence, but the sheer level of control. He'd tell me what clothes and make-up to wear, how to have my hair, how to walk, talk – everything. I started to think, 'Debbie, where are you? Where have you been?' But with the help and support of the mentoring team at Lone Parents, I'm finding myself and getting on my feet at last – I'm even going to college soon to study for a diploma in psychology. It's taken a long time, but I'm finally in control of my life!

Final thoughts

Fear not for the future, weep not for the past.

(Percy Bysshe Shelley)

Moving on from an abusive relationship requires considerable reserves of both physical and mental energy. It is important, therefore, not to waste your energies by wishing things had been different, by regretting the relationship or by hating your partner and thinking about revenge.

This is not to say you need to 'forgive and forget', nor is it to trivialize the pain and suffering he has caused you. But if you can accept that what has already happened cannot be changed and take comfort from the fact that you are now moving on, you will find it easier to mentally 'let go' of the anguish caused by the relationship.

You may find that you *are* able to forgive, and that the act of forgiveness is a healing experience in itself. Or you may go through a period of wanting revenge, of wanting to hurt your partner as much as he hurt you. It is natural to feel this way, but as these feelings lessen over time you'll feel calmer and more able to look forward rather than back. This may all take some time, of course, so don't beat yourself up over any negative emotions you may be experiencing: just be aware of them and try to consciously let them go.

When I first left my then husband, I thought a lot about revenge, but even in those early days I knew that this was destructive rather than constructive thinking, so I went deeper. I asked myself whether, if I could wave a wand that would make my ex suffer as I had for all those years, I would do it. The answer was no, of course not; what purpose would it serve? It wouldn't change what had happened, would it? No matter how badly he'd treated me, did I really want to put any human being through what I'd been through? I then considered the notion of regret. If I hadn't married him, I would have spared myself years of misery, fear and hopelessness. But on the other hand, I wouldn't have my two wonderful children either, so how could I possibly regret the marriage?

> Regret is an appalling waste of energy; you can't build on it; it is only good for wallowing in.
>
> (Katherine Mansfield)

Also, though no-one would choose to go through what I or any of the other women quoted in this book have been through, our experiences make us who we are today: stronger, more resilient women, women who have faced and overcome challenges, more confident, more aware of our own strengths and able, at last, to enjoy life and look forward rather than dreading each new day.

New relationships

Many of the women interviewed for this book were in no hurry to form a new relationship. Some even said, 'Never again – I'm staying single from now on,' or 'All men are the same, so why bother?' Conversely, some had had two or three abusive relationships, indicating that, far from feeling that all men are the same, they hoped that next time around they'd get a 'good one'. Many others had found happiness in new relationships and could hardly believe the daily joy of their new lives.

It may be a good idea to allow some 'healing time' after an abusive relationship, time in which you can rebuild your confidence and self-esteem as well as helping your children to settle in their new life. This can be a very rewarding stage because it's probably the first time you have been able to do the things you want to do without fearing your partner's reaction. You're likely to begin to socialize more and will gradually make new friends, including male friends. Given what you've been through, it's not surprising that you feel cautious about falling in love again, so don't rush into anything. However, remember that an abusive relationship is not a normal relationship, and that not all men are 'like that'. Hopefully, after reading this book and reflecting on your own experiences and those of the other women quoted here, you will be able to recognize a potentially abusive man and avoid forming another abusive relationship in the first place. Failing that, you should at least be able to recognize the warning signs and get out quickly!

Many of the women interviewed here have, like me, formed successful and happy new marriages and relationships; they all say the same thing about their new partners – 'He's wonderful; I can't believe how lucky I am!' Luck may or may not have anything to do with it, but there is another reason: we are all quite nice people; we love, like and respect our partners, and we deserve to be loved, liked and respected in return.

Useful addresses

General

Blue Cross Head Office
Shilton Road
Burford
Oxon OX18 4PF
Tel.: 0300 777 1897
Supporter Care Team: 0300 790 9903
Website: www.bluecross.org.uk

End Violence Against Women
17–25 New Inn Yard
London EC2A 3EA
Tel.: 020 7033 1559
Website: www.endviolenceagainst
women.org.uk

Lone Parents
Website: www.lone-parents.org.uk

Provides a virtual meeting place for single lone parents.

National Association of Child Contact Centres
2nd Floor, Friary Chambers
26–34 Friar Lane
Nottingham NG1 6DQ
Tel.: 0845 4500 280
Website: www.naccc.org.uk

National Family Mediation
1st Floor, Civic Centre
Paris St
Exeter EX1 1JN
Tel.: 0300 4000 636
Website: www.nfm.org.uk

Network for Surviving Stalking
National Stalking Helpline:
0808 802 0300
Website: www.nss.org.uk

One Parent Families
Lone parent helpline: 0800 018 5026
Website: www.ncopf.org.uk

Paladin: National Stalking Advocacy Service
PO Box 64640
London SW8 9DJ
Tel.: 020 7840 8960
Website: http://paladinservice.co.uk

Paws for Kids
19 Palace St
Bolton BL1 2DR
Tel.: 01204 394842
Website: www.pawsforkids.org.uk

Charity designed to help women, children and their pets escape from a life of violence and abuse.

Refuge
Free 24-hour domestic violence helpline: 0808 2000 247 (run in partnership with Women's Aid)
Tel.: 020 7395 7700 (enquiries)
Website: www.refuge.org.uk

Relate
Premier House
Carolina Court
Lakeside
Doncaster DN4 5RA
Tel.: 0300 100 1234
Website: www.relate.org.uk

Respect
4th Floor, Development House
56–64 Leonard Street
London EC2A 4LT
Phoneline: 0808 802 4040
Men's advice line: 0808 801 0327
(for men experiencing domestic
violence and abuse)
Tel.: 020 7549 0578 (enquiries)
Website: http://respect.uk.net

Membership association to help
increase the safety of those
experiencing domestic violence
through promoting effective
interventions with perpetrators.

Reunite
PO Box 7124
Leicester LE1 7XX
Tel.: 0116 255 6234 (advice line)
Website: www.reunite.org

Provides advice for those who have
had a child abducted or who fear
child abduction.

Samaritans
Freepost RSRB-KKBY-CYJK
PO Box 9090
Stirling FK8 2SA
Tel.: 116 123
Website: www.samaritans.org

Sara Charlton Foundation
4 Bedford Row
London WC1R 4TF
Website: www.saracharlton.org.uk

**Single Parent Action Network
(SPAN)**
The Silai Centre
176–178 Easton Road
Bristol BS5 0ES
Tel.: 0117 951 4231
Website: http://spanuk.org.uk

A multiracial organization of single
parents working to improve the
lives of one-parent families in the
UK and Europe. Their dedicated
website <www.singleparents.org.
uk> is packed with information for
single parents and self-help groups.

**Women's Aid Federation of
England**
PO Box 3245
Bristol BS2 2EH
Helpline: 0808 2000 247 (domestic
violence helpline, run in
partnership with Refuge)
Tel.: 0117 944 44 11 (general
enquiries)
Website: www.womensaid.org.uk
Children and young people's
website: www.thehideout.org.uk

See below for details of domestic-
abuse websites in Scotland, Wales
and Northern Ireland.

Young Minds
Suite 11, Baden Place
Crosby Row
London SE1 1YW
Tel.: 020 7089 5050
Parent helpine: 0808 802 5544
Website: www.youngminds.org.uk

Other useful helplines and
websites

Broken Rainbow
Helpline: 0300 999 5428 or
0800 999 5428
Website: www.brokenrainbow.org.uk

For lesbian, gay, bisexual and
transgender people experiencing
domestic violence.

Child Maintenance Service or Child Support Agency
Website: https://www.gov.uk/child-maintenance

Citizens Advice Bureau
For telephone numbers, look in your local phone directory.
Website: https://www.citizensadvice.org.uk

CLS Direct Legal Service
Website: www.clsdirect.org.uk

Divorce Online
Tel. (support): 01793 211211
Website: www.divorce-online.co.uk

Provides advice, information and forums.

Domestic Abuse Helpline (Scotland)
Tel.: 0800 027 1234
Website: www.scottishwomensaid.co.uk

Domestic Abuse Helpline (Wales)
Tel.: 0808 8010 800
Website: www.welshwomensaid.org

Domestic Violence National 24-hour Helpline (England)
Tel.: 0808 2000 247
Website: www.nationaldomesticviolencehelpline.org.uk

Domestic Violence 24-hour Helpline (Northern Ireland)
Tel.: 0800 917 1414
Website: www.niwaf.org

Family Mediation Council
Website: www.familymediationcouncil.org.uk

Gingerbread
Tel. (Single Parent Helpline): 0808 802 0925
Website: www.gingerbread.org.uk

Gives support, information and advice to lone parents.

The Law Society
Tel.: 020 7320 5650
Website: www.lawsociety.org.uk

Provides lists of solicitors in your area and other information.

Lone Parent Helpline
Tel.: 0808 801 0323 (Scotland)
Website: www.opfs.org.uk/service/lone-parent-helpline

National Debtline
Tel: 0808 808 4000
Website: www.nationaldebtline.org

Further reading

Bancroft, Lundy. *Why Does He Do That? Inside the Minds of Angry and Controlling Men*, Berkley Publishing Group, 2003.

Clout, Imogen. *The Which? Guide to Divorce*, Which? Books, 2005.

Dugan, Meg. *It's My Life Now: Starting Over after an Abusive Relationship or Domestic Violence*, Routledge, 2000.

Engel, Beverley. *The Emotionally Abused Woman: Overcoming Destructive Patterns and Reclaiming Yourself*, Fawcett Books, 1992.

Evans, Patricia. *Verbal Abuse Survivors Speak Out*, Adams Media Corporation, 1994.

Evans, Patricia. *The Verbally Abusive Relationship: How to Recognise It and How to Respond*, Adams Media Corporation, 2002.

Jones, Ann. *When Love Goes Wrong – What to Do When You Can't Do Anything Right*, HarperPerennial, 1993.

Miller, Mary Susan. *No Visible Wounds*, Fawcett Books, 1995.

Neligan, Annie. *The Sleeping Warrior: Women, Self-defence and Feminism*, ReadingLasses Press, 2004.

Index